Published by
ACCORD Publishing
PO Box 2585
Santa Barbara, CA 93120
To order a copy of this book go to http://www.amazon.com
Contact the author: ginarae@ginarae.com

Creative Nonfiction

Original artwork designed by Brett Hendrickson
Photo by Richard Ayling
Book design by Kosaka Design

ISBN, printed ed. ISBN 978-0-578-01881-2

I

This book is dedicated to my family,
for giving me memories that make me laugh
and a childhood
worth writing about.

To Grandma Mary, while not a character
in this book, continues to be a major source
of inspiration for me.
All the risks I take, I take for her,
for all the risks she wished
she would have made.

*The great advantage of living in a large family
is that early lesson of life's essential unfairness.*
~Nancy Mitford

WHAT READERS ARE SAYING
ABOUT THIS BOOK

"Love the style, the humor, the sad truth...it is excellent. I have been reading bits and pieces to my husband at night, so it is like an adult bedtime story book!"

"I so enjoyed your book that I gave it to my father. He is now in the next room laughing his head off and saying, 'You have to hear this one,' to my mother."

"I read the whole book to my spouse. You had us laughing, crying, both happy tears and sad."

"The thoughts on families and how they deal with different things in life and how they come through it was touching and hilarious. Wish more families had that stamina."

"During the long travel layover, I spent my time in the airport laughing."

"This book is a real page turner, that is, once I got past the thirty chick massacre! But what a cast of characters, and so descriptive."

Acknowledgments

I thank my family for allowing me to poke fun at them without anyone taking offense (or not too much) and for signing off on the story I have written for each member of the family. Thanks, Kim Conwell, for being involved in many of my fun childhood memories. Cheers and thanks to Annaka and Sienna Bland-Abramson, who as young girls were my original audience for story telling about my family, and who laughed and gasped at all the right places.

My inspiration for writing this memoir comes first from witnessing the resiliency of my family to bounce back from disabilities and setbacks. The different focus on each family member's story illustrates unique and diverse ways of expressing ourselves in the world. Indeed, we come from a broad gene pool.

Garrison Keillor, a radio story teller extraordinaire of Lake Woebegone fame, is another source of inspiration as his charming stories celebrate the quirkiness of an ordinary life that turns out to be extraordinary after all.

Thank you, thank you, thank you, Bob Poole, my husband, who has edited this work primarily, often early in the morning before he began his own busy schedule. Thanks also to my mother Phyllis who loaned me her diaries so that I could name the guilty with accuracy.

Introduction

These stories had their beginnings when I would share my childhood memories with my young stepdaughters to fill those occasional lulls in their otherwise active lives. During these story telling times, I noticed that the more I talked about death, gore, and disgusting details, the more they moved in closer to listen. I would ask, "Okay, what category of story do you want? Animals, food, or old people?" They might say, "Animals!" Quickly I would sort through my memory bank and work up a story on the spot. That is how I came up with The Duck Story.

The story went like this. "We had six ducks, one mama duck and five baby ducks. The fur on the ducklings was fuzzy and yellow. They chirped and chirped as they followed their mama in a straight line everywhere she went. Unfortunately, mama duck liked to visit the neighbors across the highway. If she was going to cross the road safely, that meant she had to look both ways to check for traffic and waddle across when it was clear.

One day as mama and her little ducklings were crossing the road, she forgot to check for traffic and a semi-truck with eighteen wheels whooshed by. I ran up to the side of the road to see what happened. All five babies and the mama had been run over. Not just run over. They were flat as pancakes, with mama duck in the lead and all five babies following in a line. Those poor critters. I went back to get a spatula to remove them from the road and get them ready for a proper burial. It goes to show that you can never know what might happen in a day. "

My young listeners gasped over the dreadful incident. Then they would request another story from a different category. Not only did they huddle closer to listen, they requested the same stories over and over again. I recounted the same repulsive details as they hung onto every foul moment, all drawn from true events. It was from entertaining my stepdaughters with details that made them squirm that I developed an appetite for sordid stories, like one acquires the bitter taste of coffee.

For this collection of stories, interviews were held with each of my family members, except my grandmother and father who are no longer with us, to uncover and capture moments as the main character experienced and remembered them. Sometimes there was disagreement as to how things "really" happened. At those times, I took liberty to tell the story from my own point of view. Versions of what happened were also derived from my mother's diaries and my own remembrances and experiences.

As of this printing, these stories are not finished. They are the rudimentary foundation of a larger work in progress. Although they have just begun to take shape, it is time I give this stage of writing to my family as a gift, just for the sordid fun of it.

Each family member's story focuses on their unique qualities and how they contribute an important thread to the tapestry of our family fabric, as loosely held as that may be. Which brings me to thoughts on family and love.

I have a theory that some families are tight knit, some are loose knit, and some have no knitting threads holding them together at all. The stories I tell are about a family that is loose knit. In our case, loose knit means not bound by obligation, loyalty, tradition, and dogmatically followed rules of expectation like I imagine the qualities of tight knit families might possess. In contrast, members of our loose knit family are free either to participate or not in family activities, without loyalty and obligation pressuring anyone to perform outside of their true desires. Even without the pressure of duty, we still have enough knit to bring us together to simply enjoy each other's company despite times where we have let each other down in small and big ways.

This collection of short stories celebrates the ability to recover from setbacks as a valued quality to nurture in families and in ourselves. I treasure this resiliency in my family because I see many people suffering and experiencing chronic sadness and resentment because they never get over how their family did not hold up an idealized image of love and nurturing. Thomas Moore, in *Care of the Soul*, calls this attachment to the concept of the ideal family "a hygienic notion of what family should be" instead of dealing with what it is – imperfect – just like the rest of the world. He suggests that an essential part of healing and just having more fun comes from accepting our family's imperfections as a fact of life, and possibly the makings of a good story. His view is that families are a microcosm of the world. Therefore, the family unit will contain shadow, including insanity, neglect, as well as the highest level of human potential.

Sordid Stories of an Ordinary Family is a collection of mini-memoirs about my family that embrace our humanness for all that we are. My own theory that I hold near and dear to my heart is that if you can love your family, and you can have compassion for their imperfections, then you really know love.

MEET THE FAMILY

SORDID STORIES OF AN ORDINARY FAMILY

GINA WAS ALL WOUND UP

HA HA!

I WAS THE EVIL TWIN. The one who killed for sport and used betrayal and trickery as a form of entertainment. April Fools' was my favorite and most plotted day of the year, that is, aside from the holidays that offered gifts. Many people say children are innocents without guile. Apparently they didn't hang out at our house.

If my parents' genetic code predetermined looks, birth defects, and character traits, what did my morally misguided side say about them? Putting moral issues aside for now, research shows that from eighteen months on, siblings know how to hurt as well as comfort each other. Children find creative ways to deal with circumstances, which, in a large unsupervised family of seven children can come in very handy.

Children also measure themselves in relation to their siblings. "Who am I?" in-comparison to my twin who was nearly blind; another sister with a severe limp who also was nearly blind; one sibling with an extra rib in the left shoulder; one with a lisp; one with red hair and fair skin, an asset if you flaunt it but deadly when overexposed to the sun; and our lone baby brother with massive freckles, which may not truly be a disability unless you hate them.

Then there was me. I was all wound up. Sudden floods of energy surged through my skinny body. A feeling of pressure would build up, resulting in the urgent need to get-up-and-go. The problem was — to do what? Running around, looking for something to amuse me, I definitely NEEDED A FOCUS. Restless with an itch that had to be scratched, one day I went down to the neighbor's yard to see what adventure could be explored. Sure enough, I found it.

The cute little chicks skittered around in circles. Their constantly moving stick legs propelled them forward, like windup toys that never stopped. The water ladle was hanging up on a nail by the well faucet. With the handle of the dipper clutched in my hand, I strode over to the first peeping baby chick with yellow fuzz and wondered what would happen if I bonked it on the head. Clunk! Nearby was another scampering chick. Clunk! And then another teetered into view. Clunk! After awhile, not a living thing was moving. All thirty chicks were lying still and on their sides in the neighbor's yard, like they were asleep. The moving target game was finally over. With nothing left to do to entertain myself, I hiked up to the rabbit cage to see what they were up to. Noticing that the little furry creatures were quietly nestled into a dark corner, I cooed to them gently and slowly opened the door so as not to scare them. Eyeing their food bowl, I gingerly picked up a few compact nuggets of alfalfa and put one in my mouth. The pellet was crunchy and green tasting. From the moisture of my mouth the crunch softened into chewy pulp. My hand scooped up a handful of the round hard cylinders and I munched more of the rabbits' breakfast. "I could be happy being a rabbit and living on this food," I thought. Not bad snacks for a hungry five year old. When all the pellets were eaten, I stroked the rabbits' soft fur, touched their twinkling noses, closed the door, and then strolled home full and satisfied.

That evening, the neighbor lady returned home to feed the baby chicks so they could grow up and pop out eggs everyday. Just as she went to throw the seeds on the ground, she stared at the rigid bodies and found the water dipper suspiciously lying by the rabbit cage. "Raccoons tend to eat their prey and they definitely don't carry water dippers around, so this full scale massacre must be the handiwork of a human," she said to her husband. She stomped up to our house and burst into the door to root out the culprit. Being the only one in the house, I was the first to be confronted. "Gina," the neighbor lady asked, breathing hard, her head and hands shaking, "were you down in our yard?"

"Yes," I meekly whispered. "Why, what's wrong?" I asked sincerely. In my mind, there had been no harm done. It was just a game. Just another day in the neighborhood. The neighbor kneeled down and peered into my face to say it was wrong what I did. Very wrong. The words ricocheted off my mind. Even though I cared about the neighbor woman like she was part of my own family, I didn't understand what the commotion was all about. It couldn't be that bad. There were no drops of blood. Confused, I went to bed that night and, surprisingly, slept deeply after having spent all my energy.

The next day, just like every day, I bounced out of bed, ran downstairs looking for adventure, something to give me challenge and focus. Darting around to all corners of the neighborhood looking for something to do, I ran from sunup to darkness, scurrying to every destination, even those that were only a few yards away from each other. Once a week like clockwork, I ran through my energy cycle from high activity to fizzle, from running, jumping, climbing, exploring, experimenting with my environment, annoying my siblings, testing the limits of my body, go, go, go---to CRASH. My body would stop moving when exhaustion set in, but only when my muscles would not obey the command from my mind to keep going. When completely depleted of energy, I could feel the lights about to go out, and knew it was time to lie down, sometimes for a whole day, in complete stillness. Once my body was prone, I could not lift even an arm or wiggle a finger.

My body felt hollow, as if a breeze could whistle through my ribs. My mind was devoid of thoughts- just a blue sky with no wind, clouds, or birds. Sounds of laughter, pots and pans clanging, doors slamming, and people talking floated around me but I was not able to connect to the sounds of life with any emotional response because emotions expend energy. Lying in the quiet shadows motionless, a weak electrical current began to pulse in my veins and slowly recharge my dry cells.

After a day of stillness, an internal electro-shock jolted my mind alert. My body suddenly tensed and hummed with a high voltage buzz, signaling my muscles to move. Bolting out of bed, I ran down to the neighbor's house again, taking advantage of our neighborly open-door policy. My eyes zeroed in on a fascinating make-up box with squares of different colors. Its mystery enticed me to pick it up from the bedroom dresser and proceed to sit on the bed and mix all the colors together, spilling the powder on the white pillow cases. At the end of the day, the neighbor lady came up to our house breathing hard and shaking again. She peered into my face to look deep within my soul to see if I even had one. "Gina," she said, "I think you should stay away from our house for a few days."

Over time, my experimentations with the world became more sophisticated and began to involve strategy. One day, my twin Lisa, younger by five minutes, initiated the next adventure of wanting to start her own ant collection in our shared bedroom. We decided on taking a field trip to the ant pile in the horse pasture up the hill. For Lisa, the expedition was simply to collect ants. The idea of scooping them in a jar to take home wasn't riveting enough for me, given my bursts of high voltage energy, short attention span, and a taste for drama. The excursion needed some spice, and I found the angle that was needed to make the field trip worthwhile.

The target was younger sister Kristy. The goal was to get her to do something she wouldn't ordinarily do and would actually refuse to do under normal circumstances. I thought to myself, "I wonder what would happen if Kristy sat on the big red ant pile naked?" I realized two things. First, this would take considerable cunning and persuasion on my part, and it had to be done with her consent, or the situation would be mean and wrong. With her consent, I would be off the hook.

Instead of my usual assertiveness, I slowly walked up to Kristy and sweetly cooed to her with a soft voice, in an attempt to appear as a caring and loving sister. "Kristy," I asked, "do you want to go with Lisa and me to check out the ant pile?" She looked into my eyes with surprise at my tenderness. Caught off guard, she responded with trust and openness to my idea. Kristy stood up to go and her face beamed with the unspoken, "I must be very special."

I held her hand while we walked up the path. Lisa tagged along behind us, committed to her idea of an ant colony swarming in our very own bedroom. When we reached the huge ant pile, I allowed Kristy a minute to admire it and then proceeded with my plan. "Okay, now you need to take off your pants," I told her as I gently helped her out of them, resting my reassuring hand on her shoulder. "Now, sit on top of the ant pile," I said as I tenderly guided her to sit dead center on the ant activity. "Well," I thought, "it should be just a matter of minutes to find out what happens." In a matter of seconds, there were a few ants moving across her legs. A few seconds later her whole body swarmed with furtively crawling ants who were acting very agitated and angry. My calculations were correct as the angry red ants started biting her everywhere all at once.

Kristy jumped up, started screaming, and then crying. Luckily I brought a dish towel in case my experiment worked, and brushed them off. "I want to go home, I want to go home," she sobbed. Escorting her back was the least I could do, I thought. I held her hand on the way back home, sensing that her consent did not cleanse my hands entirely from this deed. As I opened the door, Kristy ran into our mother's arms and blubbered, "Those ants have teeffth!!!" Turning away before I got scolded, I thought, "Well, at least she felt special for a few minutes."

Then, there was April Fools' Day, a day of scheming, which tapped into my need for challenge and focus. Simple tricks amounted to creating surprises. More advanced pranks involved predicting bathroom patterns so that a booby trap could be constructed in advance. That allowed me to leave the premises and do my own thing, knowing someone would eventually walk into the ambush. Usually I started out with simple tricks and progressed from there.

Tiptoeing into my parents' bedroom and fumbling to turn on a subdued lamp on the side of the bed to give sight to do the deed, I noticed the clock hands pointed to 1 a.m. Quietly, I picked up my mother's tube of red lipstick from the dresser and prepared to move forward with my plan. My father's slumbering lips were droopy and moving in and out as he sucked deep gulps of air with each breath. Holding my breath, I leaned in close, and drew a thick uneven line of red rouge on my father's thin lips. Proudly, I stood back to admire Dad's new voluptuous mouth.

Convulsing silently from holding back the laughter, I fell to the floor and rolled around in sheer hilarity. To complete the prank, I regained enough composure to get off the floor to sprinkle a box of Grape Nuts cereal between my mother and father. Confident that the stage had been adequately set for April Fools' Day, I tiptoed away from the scene of the crime and went to bed.

The next morning I noticed that as my mother walked to the bathroom, her eyes were puffy and her mouth was turned down in a grumpy scowl. As she opened the bathroom door, she shouted to all of us children who were eating breakfast "WHOEVER PUT THAT CRAP IN OUR BED, JUST KNOW IT CUTS LIKE GLASS!! And it's NOT funny!"

A few minutes later my father came out of the bedroom to go to the bathroom, red smears of lipstick down to his chin. The medicine chest clicked open as he took out his shaving cream. A few seconds later he yelled, "Who the HELL did this?" Then I bounded down the hall to the bathroom and beamed a smile at him, "April Fools'!!" I announced. My parents really couldn't punish me. After all, April Fools' Day is a registered holiday on the calendar and encourages pranksters to come out of hiding and do their deeds. I was surprised that my parents didn't find more humor in my cleverness. It was funny to me. Shouldn't it be funny to them?

Then there was the annual trick performed every April Fools Day by me and my sisters with our father as the target. Ganging up on dad was good for family morale because as siblings we were equal in rank for that moment and unified for the same cause. Huddled together, we carefully selected a sour well-used dish sponge. The sponge was coated with chocolate frosting and then rolled in chocolate cake crumbs, resembling a mirror image of the dessert dad was expecting. Next to the sponge cake was a glass of horse milk. Looking closely, the liquid was grayish, translucent, lukewarm, and freshly squeezed from the udder.

We watched our father's every move after dinner. He looked at the horse milk. His hand reached for the glass. We gawked at each other and sucked in our laughter to silence it so that we could keep the trick in motion. Then he lifted the glass to his lips and took a hearty gulp. After he swallowed and put the glass down, he gagged and said, "That milk is going bad!"

We all shook violently in silent laughter, wondering if we could hold the sound in for the grand finale. Then dad took his fork to cut a piece of cake and frowned when his fork bounced off. "Gall darn," he said, "what the hell is going on here?" Then our father scraped off the frosting to uncover the blue sponge and sat back in defeat. Our laughter could not be held back any longer as it ripped through my throat and my siblings' laughter roared around the table. We reveled in our father's continued gullibility. Every year he went through the ordeal of drinking the horse milk and encountering the sponge cake. Was he dimwitted or what?

The risks got higher for me with pranks that relied on calculating when someone would most likely go to the bathroom. Given that we all need to do the job at some point, I felt certain of my trap. However, human behavior is not always predictable and success is not always guaranteed.

My hand reached for the plastic honey bear in the cupboard. Then I walked over to the bathroom, surveyed the toilet seat, and squeezed the honey bear so that it squirted ropes of golden sticky goo until the seat was totally covered in glaze. Satisfied that this honey trap was the gooiest ever, I left the room to go about my day.

Much later that afternoon, at least five hours after setting the trap, I had to go to the bathroom, number two, and right now. Without thinking, I pulled down my drawers and plopped down on the toilet seat and groaned when my behind felt the sticky goo of honey. It became clear that for all my cleverness, I fell into my own trap and became a victim of my own conspiracy. There was no one to cry to and get sympathy from since I was the one who set the booby trap.

While tricks may have been my way of equalizing power in my family and possibly creating an edge in my favor, I was beginning to sense that payback was around the corner waiting for me. In our family, revenge was best when served cold. Just as I anticipated, my comeuppance did come down on me during a spirited and highly competitive game of tag.

Running from one end of the wrap-around porch to the other, I safely eluded the sister that was 'It' during tag. However, during our scurrying, someone found time to plant a slippery banana peel in my path to ensure their advantage. In my swerving out of range of being touched as well as avoiding the ol' banana peel trick, my body continued to list to the right. My feet left the porch and floated in the air. Crash, bang, clunk, were the sounds of a perfectly executed nose dive down the stairs. Head first into the dog dish full of stale breakfast scraps. As I lifted my head, my vision blurred from the long strands of hair dripping with curdled milk and soggy swollen cornflakes.

Instead of sympathy, laughter from all six siblings and my mother who came to see what the ruckus was all about, rose in volume and echoed in my head in swells, stinging my ears. Their continued amusement in my plight hung my pride out to flap on a clothesline – all for their entertainment. Sullenly staring between clumps of cereal and rivulets of sour milk, fire shot out of my eyes.

At dinner that night, after I had cleaned up, my family was eating and talking to each other, while I kept more to myself. Then someone would look at me, snort and snicker, and then everyone burst out laughing. Bolting from the table, I ran upstairs and refused to come back until my family had the decency to keep their thoughts to themselves. Scalding tears of shame burned down my checks.

Never tiring of the same story, night after night, the dinner conversation steered back to the visual details of the dog dish encounter. For weeks, even months, their unbridled mirth still stung my pride as they recounted the incident. One sister would be eating, and then snort back a laugh as she was looking down at her plate. Then they all burst out laughing, as if group thought were contagious.

Gradually I felt a shift, like a boulder dislodging from the cold cave of my heart. The loud hum of embarrassment that rang in my ears earlier was fading and then became silent, even though my family was still snorting and snickering about my mishap.

Now that I wasn't so internally preoccupied with nursing my wounds, I started paying attention to the sound of the laughter around me. Hearty, squeezed up from the gut, erupting like a geyser. Not well behaved, nor considerate, but not mean spirited. Their eyes were not against me so much as when they looked at me, they were simply replaying the potent vision. There was no malice or harm intended. It was the sound of humor with no sympathy. They were celebrating my tragedy of an injured ego. Then I felt a small surge of laughter swell up inside of me, expand, and float out to join the laughter around me.

SORDID STORIES OF AN ORDINARY FAMILY

MY MOTHER WAS A STRIPPER

I USED TO THINK, "Why can't my mother be like other mothers?" I doubted that other mothers belted out sultry blues on family outings, had Rocky Mountain Oyster parties, or were strippers. I never saw other mothers trip and fall in candy stores and then laugh like it was the funniest thing in the world. How was I to know that having a mother of these attributes would be soul food for my own budding quirky nature?

Mom, referred to as Phyllis by the rest of the world, had pushed seven children out of her fertile womb in quick succession, once even two of us at a time. Family outings started with rounding up the children. Gathering all of us into the car at the same time was a bit like herding resistant cattle through a narrow gate and into a small corral--twelve or more squirming bodies squeezed within the confines of the long station wagon, with miniature seats in the back that lifted up from under the floor to accommodate four of the littlest passengers. We were used to being crammed together like sardines because we usually had friends or cousins who came along for the adventure too. Mom would say, "Sure, come along. What's one more when there's a herd already?"

With the authority of a drill sergeant, my mother took roll call, each of us squeaking "Here!" in turn. "Celie! Shelley! Lisa! Gina! Celie! I mean Kristy, or whatever your name is! Carol! Bud!" Roll call became a regular occurrence after she went to the dentist and forgot the kid that was supposed to go. I am not sure why that mishap ended up in the local paper.

Down the winding country gravel road we drove, eager to fill our sacks with rocks, pine cones and pillage buckets of berries from the wilderness. The car tires kicked up rocks like gun shots and clouds of dust billowed into our open windows until the air inside the car settled into a haze of silt.

Mom would start humming a few notes to herself, then moved into outright singing at full throttle. We chimed in with the usual round of "Michael Row The Boat Ashore, HALLELUJAH," round after round after round until we didn't care about Michael and his stupid boat any more.

With vocal chords all warmed up, I watched my mother's eyes glow with desire and her lips purse as if she were receiving a kiss as she transitioned from singing children's songs to a sultry malt liquor rendition of "Swing Low, Sweet Chariot, COMING FOR TO CARRY ME HOME. I looked over Jordan and what did I see. COMING FOR TO CARRY ME HOME. Swing Low, Sweet Chariot. COMING FOR TO CARRY ME HOME." She hit the low notes with a growl and hung onto tones like a seductress with pent up passion yearning for release. We children recognized our puny voices could not keep up with her rapture and quieted down to watch our red-headed Norman Rockwell Mother turn into Queen of Soul Aretha Franklin. That gravelly, raw voice should have alerted me that this was only a small sample of what was to come.

We didn't have long to wait. Late that summer, the ranch next door was castrating bulls and was about to have an abundance of Rocky Mountain Oysters, Mom's name for bulls' balls. My parents decided to capitalize on the bounty and have a Rocky Mountain Oyster party. Can't let those go to waste.

A slew of liquor bottles lined the kitchen counter ready for action, accompanied by maraschino cherries and little onions to adorn drinks. Carrot and celery sticks were precisely stacked like neat rows of posts on plates. Perfectly scalloped rounds of Jell-O (jiggling with a little prodding from my fingers) offered treasures in each bite of fruit cocktail or shredded carrots and raisins suspended in translucent green space. My eyes were scanning the scene, trying to find incriminating evidence, even though I was deathly afraid of finding what I was looking for. No sign of the main course, yet.

Before the party, I asked my mother, "How do you cook this kind of dish? Will you serve it as two full mounds of meat? You know, so that they resemble the truth of what they really are?" "Oh no, Honey," my mother chuckled as she glanced at my furrowed brow. "They will be sliced thin and people can dip them in various sauces." She leaned over to my ear and softly disclosed, "The secret ingredient for this dish is sage." "Right," I retorted with my best sneer.

As time grew near, Mom ordered me in a stern voice - the kind that lets a dog know it's about to be punished - to stay upstairs with my sisters and little brother. "Under no circumstances are you to come downstairs and interfere with my evening. And absolutely no whining or tattling." Believe you me, staying away was easy. There was no way I was going to associate with people who ate testicles. I don't care what fancy name you call them. In my judgment, everyone who attended, particularly my parents, was DISGUSTING BE- YOND REDEMPTION.

From the upstairs window, I watched the guests arrive, all frisky and randy with off color jokes. No doubt, they anticipated the aphrodisiac qualities of Rocky Mountain Oysters. Cocktail glasses clinked. The air was filled with raucous laughter and the smells of cooking oil, salt and pepper, and the meaty smell of bulls' nuts well done. Try as I might, I couldn't hear any comments, good or bad, about the meal, so I reluctantly pulled my ear away from the knot hole in the wooden stairs that provided a listening post into my parents' bedroom and other downstairs activities.

The next morning, there were no signs of leftovers, not even tidbits of meat pushed to the side of the plate by the less courageous partygoers. Only drained bottles of liquor, forgotten drinks with onions that sunk down to the bottom of the glass and cleanly scraped dishes piled high. The evening that I painfully endured ended up with an ordinary stack of dishes. In just a few days I got over my trauma and life with my mother went back to normal, or so I thought.

A few months later, Mom got out her Singer Slant-o-Matic 401 sewing machine, a leader in its time with lots of fancy options for embroidery, button holes, darning, and scalloping edges. For the time being, she postponed her laundry and cleaning routine and focused on sewing an outfit for a special occasion. Hovering close to her side, I watched her unfold the bolt of lime green, lemon yellow and magenta striped fabric with some satin threads mixed in for texture and shine.

Sewing pins stuck out like a row of porcupine quills from between her voluptuous lips, lips that felt like pillows when I kissed them. She pulled the pins from her puckered mouth, one by one, and attached the pattern to the fabric. Her fingers clutched the scissor handles and made quick work of cutting out the dress and pinning the pieces together. Without once lifting her eyes off her project, my mother hunched over the fabric as it moved through the feet of the sewing machine inch by inch until PRESTO, it hung together as a dress.

When it was time for the finishing touches, she stuffed a whole bag of foam rubber into the breast area until the bosom was larger than any cup size known to mankind. Anyway, I hoped so. Her hands caressed the fabric as she hand stitched the red ball fringe around the nipple area and the hem. "Ooohh la la! This is my 'Lola' dress," she said. I learned later that "Lola" was her stage name for her upcoming stripping performance titled "Fringe Benefits" for the Ladies Bowling Tournament Banquet.

Dress rehearsal amounted to Lola sucking in her belly as she pulled up the zipper, tucking herself in firmly, and swinging the red fringe provocatively in midair. My oldest sister Celie ran up the stairs to see what was happening, appraised her alluring silhouette, and said, "Boy, those big boobs sure make your waist look little." "Honey," Mom said, "the reality is that I'm a brood sow. And I'm going to show these women what a plump and clumsy stripper really looks like."

When the stripping music blared, she started the entertainment behind the changing screen, as her hand flung various underwear garments over the top of the partition--a slip, a girdle, and a very large bra. The stunned audience wondered if she had anything left on, or better yet, what she might have to offer. With the tension high, Lola, with a platinum blonde wig and silk red rose between her teeth, came out from behind the screen in her fancy new dress, bulky hips swiveling, bumping, and grinding.

Lola bumped and grinded her way through the rows of tables with the fringe of red balls jumping and swaying. She fumbled for her zipper on the back of her dress. Grabbing and missing, the zipper never quite came down. All the better to tease the audience that she just might do it.

The spectators started to get into the game and took playful grabs at her plump curves that squeezed into the tight dress. She lunged out of their grasps and swayed those hips in a defiant gesture of "You can look, but you can't touch." At the end of the song, Lola sashayed back to the changing screen with a flirtatious last look over her shoulder and tossed the red rose to the ecstatic crowd, signaling the end of the Lady's Bowling Tournament Banquet.

For a few weeks after the event, my mother was approached by everyone she met. Someone walked by us in the grocery store and said, "Have you seen Lola lately? That gal is really stacked." Embarrassed at any mention of my mother and sexuality in the same sentence, I quickly excused myself and ran to the dairy section for a gallon of milk.

News about Lola spread like a virus to neighboring towns and professional associations. She was asked to demonstrate her charms again for the Four State Convention of Mayors that was going to be held in our small town. My father, who normally liked randy jokes and exchanged them freely, put his foot down on this one. "No wife of mine is going to be seen in that dress entertaining a bunch of mayors as if you were a---- a--- loose woman!!!" So far the family name included outlaws, poachers, wild musicians, womanizers, and my uncle, the beloved local sheriff. Given that I came from a family that straddled both sides of the law, we didn't have much reputation to gain or lose.

My mother retreated from her fleeting time as a local celebrity. Rather than smudge our already tarnished family name, she packed the Lola dress away in a remote drawer. To subdue the dress into so small an area, Mom had to press down hard on the bosom while I shut the drawer slowly as she eased her hands out. Lola was successfully restrained into her small confines away from public viewing. Unfortunately, when the drawer was accidentally opened by a careless child, she popped out and had to be wrestled back in the same way.

With Lola securely stowed away, my mother refocused her energy on tackling the mountain of laundry and cleaning the house, knowing it would be undone five minutes after we were home from school. In addition, she resumed cooking and being the hostess for regular bouts of company who dropped by for coffee and to talk the day away. By October of that year, she counted 3,000 visitors. Since we lived by the side of the main road, it was convenient for visitors to drop in, sometimes the same squatters two or three times a day. On and on they droned about whether blue was a good color to paint their kitchen or why they took back their lying and cheating husband.

One day Mom was getting ready to tackle the pile of mending and saw the most frequent squatter drive up in her car and waddle toward the door. People-tired and desperate for uninterrupted time, Mom ran and hid in the small cramped bathroom. The neighbor opened the front door without knocking and tromped around the house like she owned the joint, looking for my mother in every room, calling out her name. This was her third visit today. I overheard my mother say once that this neighbor's presence was like a Staph infection that wouldn't go away. I could see by the way Mom inhaled cigarettes during those visits that the pus was starting to fester in her heart.

A prisoner in her own home, Mom held her breath, sitting on the toilet, hoping the visitor would give up and retreat. The neighbor swung open the bathroom door and exclaimed, "Phyllis! What are you doing in here?" "Taking a shit," my mother said flatly. In essence, life went back to normal.

However, one summer Lola came out from hiding and made a charismatic encore in front of hundreds of viewers during our July parade. Lola, on behalf of our 4-H Club, provided a social service by picking up manure after the horses pranced through the small town streets. She wielded a shovel and attitude while picking up road apple after road apple, as the parade crawled through town. There she was, sweating under the blonde wig in the high noon sun, a smoldering cigarette held between her sneering red lips, her bosom pointing to the crowd. No swiveling, bumping, or grinding this time. Instead, her movements consisted of scooping, lifting, and heaving. She was the perfect ending to an otherwise predictable parade. My mother's stripper days were over, but not her charms.

DAD NEEDED SOME LUCK

WHEN A MAN GETS DOWN on his luck, he can try to correct the course through hard work and then maybe he will receive good fortune. When he tries to correct the course and is still down on his luck, he can work even harder and longer hours, into the evenings and through the weekends. This was my father. However, when that didn't work, he used hope for fuel to keep him motivated to continue on. Eventually the wishful thinking of hope became the substitute for good fortune. My father's enterprise, known as Four Mile Post and Pole, offered wood products from fence posts to poles to lumber. Rows and rows of white wood piles glared in the sun, turning grey over the years, ready for customers to buy, as my father waited for his luck to change. When his post and pole fortune didn't materialize, Dad started to search for abundance elsewhere in equally elusive pursuits. And then, finally, he struck gold. Darkness had set in a couple of hours ago and so did our appetites. "Dinner can wait until your father finishes his work," said Mom. From our dining room window we children clustered together and peered out to watch him work in the post yard, which was just beyond the postage stamp of our backyard. Staring, our eyes barely blinked, as if focusing on his every move would create enough gravitational pull to entice him to sit at the dinner table sooner.

Like twin moons, the headlights of dad's tractor bounced and bobbed under the strain and heavy weight of the bundle of posts clutched in its front-end forks. The bright moons stopped moving. Thud. Another bundle of posts landed on the bed of a semi-truck. The tractor backed down the ramp and roared away to scoop up another bundle and another and another until the semi-truck drove away into the night filled with the maximum load.

When the tractor stopped moving and the lights dimmed into darkness, we clutched our soup spoons, ready for action. The second Dad finally sat at the dinner table, my mother quickly filled his bowl. Immediately the clang of spoons began as we dug into our beef stew, tore off pieces of homemade bread, and eagerly eyed the plum topsy turvy pudding.

Dad chewed a few bites and then said, "I found

a stack of poles that I'd forgotten about that have been sitting around for a couple of years. I'm going to bring 'em up to the front of the post yard so that they get sold before the others." The only response was our slurping of juicy stew. "I'm thinking that a lumber mill here could diversify our operations," he continued. Just who was he talking to? We all looked at each other to see whose job it was to respond. Where exactly would I, being a self-absorbed child, take a conversation about diversifying operations and how would I elaborate on the lumber topic, especially with food being the most important topic in my mind right now?

Nonetheless, after looking down into my bowl of brown broth, stirring the potatoes and carrots around the tender pieces of beef, and taking a swig of cold milk, I thought I'd take a stab at dinner conversation and forced out some cheerful conversation, "OKAY, HOW MANY POSTS ARE WE GOING TO EAT TONIGHT?" Dad jerked his head up and put down his spoon. "Damn, that reminds me. I need to check on the load of wood in the treating tank. Got to make sure the pressure is high enough so that the creosote gets all the way through the wood."

His chair screeched on the floor when he pulled back from the table. "I'll be back as soon as you can shake a stick," he assured us as he headed out the door. "No Dad, don't go," daughter Kristy whined, playing up her role as Daddy's little girl, pleading with her round green eyes and looking up at just the right angle with her best pout to snag his heart. "Honey," Dad said, "I wish I didn't have to go. If only my hired hand could get out of jail long enough to put a load of wood through the tank so I could sit here with you. But he is behind bars serving time for stupidity, so I have to go. I'll be back before you know it."

Sure enough, he was good for his word. Dad slid his chair up to the dinner table just as we started our second helping. Our heads bowed over the bowls, with a posture designed to efficiently take the brimming spoons to our mouths in the least amount of time and effort. Just as Dad resumed eating his cold bowl of stew, Kristy contributed to the post and pole conversation and asked, "DAD, ARE YOUR POSTS BAKED YET?"

Years ago, the back yard was larger and created physical and mental space between home and work. Gradually the rows of posts crept closer and closer to our house each year until, from the back porch, we could almost jump on a stack of posts. When one of us decided it was time to see Dad for some one-on-one time, we would amble down to the post and pole yard, an easy walk since it was just a few feet away from the back door of our house. Standing in his line of sight, with hopeful stares we looked into his face as he drove by. He always stopped and smiled and plunked his little companion on top of the filthy chains in the box behind the tractor seat where he sat.

When we got older and desired quality time, we outgrew asking for permission and marched up to the tractor with a sense of entitlement that the ride was ours to be had. As soon as he stopped, one of us hopped on and stood to the side of our father. The wind whipped our hair around as we clung to the top of the huge fender. We looked contentedly ahead, like a dog leaning into being scratched in his favorite spot. We basked in the roar and bumpy lurching of the tractor as we accompanied Dad transporting bundles of post and poles and stacking them in long and high rows.

One day, Mom looked out of the dining room window while folding a stack of freshly-laundered jeans, counting sixteen pair in all. Her eyes caught hold of the glare of white posts and noticed that another row was creeping into the grass area of the side yard. She sipped her coffee and shared her thoughts with the neighbor lady across the table, "Pretty soon we will be storing posts in the kids' bedroom upstairs! I think I need to get my husband away from the yard before he starts talking about posts for pillow talk and foreplay." The neighbor lady joked, "Hey, at least you know where your husband is!" My mother poured another cup of coffee for her and the neighbor and sighed, "I certainly do know where he is. I can look out the window and see him anytime I want."

Mom knew that pleading, whining, and playing the sympathy card as a strategy for getting livelier topics of conversation at the dinner table--never mind a much needed vacation--would not work on my father. His struggle for getting ahead or from falling too far behind set precedence over everything. Work was his trump card. Besides, he was regularly short handed, as he had to fire those whose incompetence imposed a severe liability. Workers that had drinking problems weren't reliable either and usually left on their own so they could pursue the bottle full time.

One day, Mom was feeling restless and said to Dad, "Hey, how about let's get away from here?" He looked up from his coffee cup, and checked out the post yard, like a guard scans the area for signs of movement. Mom knew that his resistance to the idea of leaving his watch and missing a much needed sale was as certain as the loud bang a screen door makes when it is slamming shut. She added, "Let's go for a drive and look at other post yards." Bingo! Spying on other successful operations always convinced Dad to leave his watch because now a drive with Mom was time well spent. A rare moment, just the two of them, meandering around other post yards to see how different businesses made a go of it. Dad whispered to Mom as they got out of the car and proceeded toward a yard, "You and I are posing as rich farmers who could be potential buyers. That way they will reveal their trade secrets. So, don't go asking too many informed questions."

The tours revealed more mystery and questions than answers. The question that persistently nagged my father was, "How do other yards with smaller lots and less inventory and men who seem to him to be working in slow motion have the knack of bringing in $75,000 a month? Why, that's more than I bring in a year!"

After one of these tours of a successful and booming enterprise, I noticed Dad sitting slumped in his easy chair which was already sunken in the seat from many previous hours of contemplating finances. His grimy work boots sprawled on the equally broken down foot rest. His eyes stared straight ahead, engaged in a conversation we could not hear. I imagined his mind was a cog of wheels that were smoking and groaning from the friction of movement without lubricant, trying to grapple with the reality that putting in long days, nights, and weekends, as well as piling up the most inventory of all the yards was not turning out to be the recipe for profit and getting ahead of the game. This is not what the American dream promised its hard working and honest citizens.

A few days later, it was morning again and a new day. Optimistically, Dad proclaimed, "Another day, another dollar," as he sipped his third cup of coffee, waiting for the caffeine jolt to take hold and give him the ambition he needed for another long day in the yard. Gazing at the red and white checked vinyl tablecloth, Dad breathed deeply and downed the last of his coffee.

He glanced out the window, noticing that the sun had slipped behind the newly forming clouds. A rain storm was brewing. The wind was picking up, hurling leaves, a card board box, and plastic toys into the air and throwing them against the house. A dust cloud swirled low to the ground and a sudden gust furled the grey dirt into the air as it moved down the road. Watching the commotion,

Dad said, "It seems that the wind blows all the good luck and breaks to others and just leaves me in the dust." Mom grumbled, "If anyone asked me about going into the post business, I'd tell them that they're sure to sign up for ten years of poverty and many years of hard labor." He didn't notice her gesture of solidarity. His blue eyes kept staring ahead, rarely blinking. Apparently he was talking more to himself than sharing his pain with her.

For whatever financial abundance may have evaded my father he made up for it by keeping my mother pregnant- with hopes of spawning a son. "I heard that fertility for women drops after the age of twenty six," he said to my mother. "You're twenty eight. We had better get at it if we are going to get our son."

Soon after that conversation, my mother's fertile abilities soon blessed my father with a fifth daughter. The little girl crawled over his lap and took naps in the crook of his arm. He lifted her up over his head and thrilled at her excitement over heights and her daddy's love. He smiled back at his bounty. A few years later, my father produced more abundance. The sixth child was born, also a daughter.

Our coffee pot was constantly percolating a new batch of brew, reported to be the strongest in the county-a truism since it percolated all day and was always ready for country hospitality. One day a neighbor man stopped by for a cup, finding Dad sitting in his easy chair holding the latest new born while the rest of us girls ran in and out of the house. In a man-to-man moment away from ear-shot of the girls, the neighbor said to my father, "You know, Everett, I have four boys and that is enough for me. If you keep trying to have a son, you might have to make a dozen girls first! Are you up for that kind of risk?" "Ha, ha, ha, ha," they both chortled at the gamble Dad was playing.

A few years later, Mom and Dad stole away from us long enough to attend a party up the road a few miles. Frivolous socializing, other than neighbors dropping in for coffee, was an infre-quent occurrence. We children chimed in unison, "We want to come! We want to come!" Mom said, "I really can't take all you kids to this party tonight. In fact, I can't take you to any civilized people's homes and expect to be invited back. Even though we take in other people's kids more times than I care to count, we can't expect others to take ours." The reality was, family invitations were extremely rare.

Swirling the ice cubes in a potent elixir of rum and coke, a man with drink in hand, sidled up to Dad and said, "Everett, how are you doing with all those females in your house and being the only man? What, can't you make a boy? You know, don't you, that it's up to the man to make the boy happen."

"Well, it ain't easy being the only man," Dad said, appreciating the acknowledgment of his plight. "I haven't been able to get in the bathroom without an appointment for a month. And when

I do get in there, I have to wade through the bras and panties. Boy, they sure do like to chatter at the dinner table. And they go on and on about nothing important. Now, if I had some boys, I bet it would be quieter at the dinner table. Oh well. Hey, at least I know that my willy works and that I'm not shooting blanks!"

The man, flushed in the cheeks with yet another freshly downed rum and coke, licked his slack lips which started to hang down from the weight of high octane alcohol and said, "Since I've got a few sons of my own, I have some advice for you, Everett." His voice lowered and my father leaned closer to the man with the answers, "In order for you to get a son, you should become a 'swinger'. You know what a swinger is, don't you?" Before Dad could truly consider the answer, the man blurted out the punch line, not being able to hold back any longer. "It is a man who doesn't wear underwear! Maybe that will get you a son! You know what that means don't you? No more of those snug fitting Fruit of the Looms. Got to go back to those boxers where you can hang loose!" Swirling his drink so that the ice cubes clinked, the man took a swig and yelled over the growing noise of the party, "I hear the position can make a difference too! You know, all fours. Heh heh heh heh. We're not good swimmers, so you got to put a lot of them in there, as deep as you can. Heh heh heh heh."

A few years later, my mother became pregnant with the seventh child. The headline news of the birth rang through the countryside, a trophy of an eight pound twelve ounce boy. At long last, my father's son was born. Dad's luck did change. His long sought after abundance was granted, at least in his personal life. While eeking out a living remained his constant challenge, his gold was his son. Now, having found his bounty, he didn't have to keep my mother pregnant, for he had attained his destiny as a truly fulfilled parent and prosperous man.

SORDID STORIES OF AN ORDINARY FAMILY

CALAMITY CELIE

ALMOST ALL OF MY SIBLINGS were born with either a birth defect, developed a disability, barely escaped death, or encountered some tragedy. Celie, the first born, was blessed with all of them. It all started when a truck that was hauling post and poles drove out of the yard and ran over Celie with the left front wheel and broke her leg. Unbeknownst to the driver, the little toddler followed him out of our house and was hanging onto the front bumper for fun when the vehicle sped forward. Celie's chubby fingers let go and her body was pinned beneath the front tire. The driver felt his tire rise up unexpectedly. Sensing that something was wrong, he decided on a hunch to back up and check things out, saving her short little life. Celie's numerous near brushes with death and encounters with disabilities may read like a repeat offender's rap sheet, but did not break her spirit or slow her down.

Once Celie's broken leg healed, she had only a few uneventful years before Mother Nature kicked in and took away most of her eyesight. I tugged at Mom's sleeve to get her attention and asked, "Why does Celie wear glasses that make her eyes look big?" Mom said, "Well, Celie had a white film grow over her eye that needed to be removed so that she could see. That white film is called a cataract. The doctors removed the film that covered Celie's eyeball with a knife, like peeling a layer off an onion. Later she had to have a needle stuck in her eyes to get rid of the rest of the film. Even though the film is gone, so is part of the lens of her eyes. Her glasses are thick so she can see."

Those thick magnifying glasses, Celie's only window to the world, confined her to seeing the world through tunnel vision. If something wasn't dead center right in front of her, she couldn't see it. One day Celie was staring off into space chasing some thought in her head. Mom was talking to her and wasn't able to get her attention. "Celie, are you deaf?" Mom yelled. Indignant, Celie quickly retorted, "I may not see so good, but at least I can hear!"

In truth, the rest of the world ceased to exist while Celie focused on trying to really see something, especially if her environment was not familiar. Everything was so magnified, so large, most things were a blur. The intensity of her concentration created a power drain from other parts of her body and shut off her ability to hear. When she determined she had visually identified the object of her attention, presto, her hearing came back.

Then dear ol' Mother Nature dealt another card. During a check up monitoring Celie's broken leg from a few years before, the doctor informed Mom and Dad that signs of polio were found in her deformed collarbone. During the next few years, when the rest of us were growing tall and strong and running around the countryside like wild bobcats, Celie's left leg gradually became weaker and started shrinking. The tendon on her left polio-ridden leg slipped to the wrong side of the foot and had to be rerouted to the back of the heel. When the doctors cut through the gristle of her heel, they found that blood did not circulate to aid in the healing, and part of it had died. "She is lucky, the doctor told my parents. "Her whole heel could have died. It is important to count your blessings." Part of her heel had to be cut off to save the part that still had blood flow. The remaining back of her foot, the part she needed to be thankful for, shriveled and had sunken in places, like a flat tire.

It seemed that every summer when the rest of us rode horses, morning, noon, and night, played Cowboys and Indians, and devoured as many chocolate fudge popsicles as our stomachs could hold, Celie would spend her summer vacation in the children's ward at the hospital for yet another surgery on her legs.

One summer, the doctor shortened the bone in her good right leg one and one half inches so that it would be equal in length with her shrunken left limb, restoring her like a stool with matching legs. However, even with medical technology aimed at making her whole, Celie's gait still wobbled, particularly when running. At top speed the right leg was planted far ahead of her, creating the leverage for lunging forward, while the left leg pushed from behind.

Celie hobbled past Mom, teetering almost out of control. "What's your hurry?" my mother shouted. "Slow down or you'll hurt yourself. You'd think there was a fire in your pants." Running in shoes that were two sizes different to accommodate one dwarfed foot and one normal foot, Celie sped past ignoring the words of caution.

On her thirteenth birthday Celie got a bra and a bridle. She was thrilled with both. Although there wasn't much to put in the bra, it honored her nonetheless. The bridle was to keep her happy for the one year wait before she got a horse. When she finally had the real thing, everything was horses this, horses that. Savoring the aromas of manure and horse sweat, Celie was a full fledged horsy kind of girl.

During winter months, all of us kids took turns over who had to go out into the snow flurries to feed and water the horses and risk frost bite. When it was Celie's turn, she would throw the hay in front of the horses, scoop up her horse's hoof prints embedded in the icy snow just before leaving the pasture, and put the ice sculptures in the freezer for remembrance sake. Hoof prints alamode. Pawing through the freezer, I had to throw the frozen hoof prints to the side so I could see the food groups I was told to fetch. Some of the snow clods were grey and gritty with dirt and possibly manure. In spite of the bags of frozen corn and steaks in white butcher paper, at the end of winter the freezer did resemble a horse pasture.

Celie's free spirit, the one that refused to slow down for inconveniences such as a broken leg, polio, and cataracts, really cut loose when she rode her horse, Cactus. True to his name, he hurt those who came in close proximity to him. Cactus had an annoying habit of biting people when they weren't looking. Baring his teeth, he grabbed a hunk of skin, bit down hard, and twisted to add further injury while he had someone crying in his grips. Those who dared get close to him usually left with large round bruises. I can attest to that. Another annoying habit Cactus had was that when he smelled the fear of inexperienced riders, he bolted at a dead run, crashing through thickets of tress and low hanging branches with the soon-to-be casualty clinging to his neck in terror of dying a premature death. Cactus was good to Celie though, a reprieve she well deserved.

Although Celie's power base may not have been on the ground, put her on a horse with four strong legs and she turned into a stealthy barbarian that would have made Attila the Hun proud. Feeling her oats, she crowed, "YEEHAW!!" as she galloped past us sisters, kicking up a dust cloud, and forcing us to run and find a place to hide. "YEEEEEHAAAWWWW you little chicken shits!!!!" she whooped with savage intensity. Once, while circling back to kick up some more trouble, she leaned over the side of her horse to whap a sister with the ends of the leather reins, lost her balance, fell off, and broke her pelvis.

Despite seeing only what was directly in front of her (that was if she was paying attention) and the fact that the trees, grass, and landscapes were a blur, Celie refused to let such minor setbacks slow her down. One sleigh riding season, she sledded down the hill called the Nutcracker, chasing after boys as usual, going lickitly split. The Nutcracker got its name because boys were never the same after they slammed into the last dip, a depression in the hillside that had gotten deeper and more treacherous over the years. "Look out below!!!" Celie yelled as she bounced over the bumps and flew down the hill. In a daring attempt to run some boy over, she didn't see the swing set looming ahead and smashed her sled into one of the poles.

Hunched over on the sled cradling her arm, she swayed back in forth in the fetal position. Celie's snow encrusted form blended in with the whiteness of the hill. Her lips were blue and numb from the cold. A slight trickle of blood was running down at the corner of her scowling mouth.

From where I stood, it sounded like she was whimpering something about "Shit, Shit, Shit." Being the oldest sister, Celie had a more developed vocabulary than the rest of us. With her thick glasses completely fogged over and hair clotted with lumps of snow, Celie ran into the one room school house we attended, located at the bottom of the sleigh riding hill. She waved and flapped her injured arm in the teacher's face and shouted over and over, "I was riding down the hill and it was like the swing set pole reached out and grabbed me! I think I broke my arm! I think I broke my arm! I think I broke my arm!" as if the first or second report was not enough to convince our school teacher of the severity of the situation.

The teacher turned away from Celie's dramatic gestures to grade her stack of papers. The school kids went back to their conversations. I came in from the cold and was embarrassed at Celie flapping her arm and causing such a ruckus, so I pretended she wasn't talking. She kept waving her arm until the teacher reached over for the phone to call Mom, more as a way to get rid of the nuisance than as a medical response. Mom, who was busy with household chores and visiting neighbors, was similarly skeptical as to the gravity of the situation. After a long pause on the phone, Mom relented when the teacher suggested she take Celie home. "Okay, send her home," Mom said, suspecting that the drama of the contrived situation was conjured up to gain attention.

Part of the unwritten and unspoken survival guide for living in our large family was that in order for an injury to be taken seriously, we had to be lying in a pool of blood with a limb sheared off or barely hanging on by a few ligaments. Injuries had to be visible and severe in order to qualify for nurturing in our household. "If you are crying loudly, you can't be too hurt," Mom said. In spite of there being no visual signs of blood to support that the injury was for real, Celie convinced Mom that the situation was worth looking into. Apparently, Celie's repetitive phrases punctuated with a whine and high pitch could wear even the most reluctant person down.

The doctor confirmed that her wrist was indeed broken by saying, "She's lucky she only broke her wrist." Once again, misfortune helped us count our blessings because we got to acknowledge that it could have been worse. However, sickness was not something to be nursed or doted on by Mom, in case we would find and invent things in which to whine and get sick about. Therefore, sympathy was given to Celie sparingly and was short lived, if given at all. Another unwritten and unspoken rule of the household was that, "Thou shall attain independence and self sufficiency as early as possible. So, fend for yourself."

Soon thereafter, yearning to expand her radius of adventure, Celie started wondering what was out there besides the horse pasture and sledding hills. It was time for Celie, with her tunnel vision and speedy tendencies, to get behind the steering wheel of a car and check things out.

Once she figured out the brakes and clutch and gas, she was ready to drive the four miles to town to show off her wheels. Not much happening that day on Main Street, so she headed back home. Just as she was turning onto Dead Man's Corner, a sharp blind corner on top of a hill, the hood of the Ford Pinto flew up and crashed into the windshield. Tires screeched as she hit the brakes, leaving a long stretch of rubber on the road as the car careened between the right lane and the left lane, flirting with both ditches.

Celie craned her neck out the window to see around the hood and lurched the car to safety on the side of the road. After a neighbor who had witnessed the fishtailing of the car checked to see if Celie needed help, she drove home the rest of the way, alive and cheery, and totally unconcerned by the mishap. When Mom saw the hood taped down to the body of the car and the cracked windshield and heard her daughter's cheerful recalling of the near brush with tragedy, she threw her arms up in the air and exclaimed, "It will be a miracle, Celie, if you live to graduate from high school!" The very next day Celie skidded to a stop on the gravel driveway. Witnessing this, Mom thought to herself, "God, please protect us all on the highway."

With the addition of cars, and the speed that could take Celie places she never dreamed of in the horse pasture, her world became much more socially expansive. Celie soon discovered the wonders of beer, late nights, cowboys, outlaws, rednecks, loggers, farmers, musicians, artists, and complete strangers. She befriended them all. Just because some had a long criminal record did not mean they were not nice people. Celie reasoned that rap sheets are like disabilities. You don't need to feel bad about them and they do not have to slow you down.

"Celie, sometimes I wonder if you think you have to drink all the beer in the county before it gets outlawed!" Mom said as she saw the empty cans piled high in the back seat of her car from the last social outing. Over time, with her carousing ways, keeping company with men on the fringes of a moral society, and an unapologetic wild spirit, Celie became known to our town as Calamity Jane.

Celie smiled through all her hardships, including those self imposed, and maintained her loveable, magnetic, and sunny disposition. People in our small town smiled back at her and recognized her beauty, even if she didn't. She was blind to the fact that attractiveness can transcend a limp and thick glasses. Her toothy grin glinted with hints of the angel and devil. Not the evil one that sinners are afraid of. This devil of hers was more uninhibited than mean spirited. As Lyle Lovett's song goes, "She wasn't good, but she had good intentions."

GRANDMA LILY'S BIRD BATH

EACH TIME GRANDMA LILY delivered a child, she got bigger-- and bigger-- and bigger. By the time the twelfth baby slid out from her womb, she was almost as round as she was tall. I saw her regularly, mostly because her snowy white hair was cut and curled on a weekly basis by my mother. Once the rollers were taken out, the curls combed back and hair sprayed, the final effect was that she looked like our first president George Washington. Most importantly was how she changed my view of the world the day I helped her take a bath.

Grandma Lily lived up the road in a blue house that could be seen from our dining room window. I was never sure why she went to all the trouble to take baths at our house. Perhaps she needed to get away from my grandfather. His motto was, "If you give a woman one darn thing, she'll start thinking she needs more." There were no signs of closeness between my grandparents, with her bedroom being at one end of the house and his at the other. How they got close enough to conceive twelve children I will never know.

It was much later I found out that only eleven children were actually conceived by Grandma Lily. The twelfth child under her wing was actually a long standing family secret. When I found out that that my uncle was really my cousin, it seemed very normal. I had seen our cat allow a new born puppy to suckle its nipple along side the kittens, so I knew that taking care of babies that weren't your own was part of nature. However, when the child found out his sister was his mother, and his mother was his grandmother, I imagine it felt about as normal as lightening ripping through a tree.

As a child, there were many things you never knew for sure about adults. All I saw was that my grandfather's face was blank with no sign of anything going on inside while my grandmother's face twitched with spasms. Her eyes fluttered at the corners and blinked wide open and shut tight involuntarily. When she smiled, the corners of her mouth jittered. Her eyebrows repeatedly arched up and down, up and down, as if they couldn't find their right place.

Grandma Lily stood out from our household of heathens by being a Seventh Day Adventist.

There were dietary rules she went along with that followed God's plan of living the good and pure life. She followed them, that is, until she didn't. "Oh no, I can't eat ham," she said at large family dinner gatherings as she passed on steaming plates of meat to others. When someone tried to encourage her to take a bite she remained firm by restating, "No, I had better not. Scripture says to stay away from unclean meat from cloven hoof like pork." Her plate had generous helpings of potatoes and vegetables and clean meat, like beef or chicken.

"Oh, here, let me take care of clearing the table and you all can just relax," she said when everyone had finished eating. Just as she entered the kitchen, most of the adults bolted for the back door so that they could have their secret cigarette, since all smoking had to be done on the sly, away from Grandma Lily's disapproving eyes.

Alone in the kitchen and thinking she was out of sight of witnesses, my devout grandmother grabbed a slice of ham from the serving plate and crammed the whole slab into her mouth, chewing and swallowing, like a bird gobbles up the worm, lest it find a way to escape. Her eyes closed as she savored every bite of the forbidden flesh. Her tongue ran the full circumference of her greasy lips to get the last morsel of flavor.

Almost barging in on her, I backed up and waited in the hallway for a few minutes to make sure Grandma Lily had her fill of secret gorging before going into the kitchen again to fetch some toothpicks for rest of the family who needed to pry some ham strands from between their teeth. "I'm going to the kitchen," I yelled to give my grandmother time to regroup. As I walked in and opened a cupboard, her head was turned to the side intently studying the weaving of a potholder in her hand as if it were the most fascinating thing she'd seen in a long time. As I glanced over at her, I could see a big wad of purple bubble gum stuck behind her earlobe, handy for the next chewing session, I guessed. At that moment she reached behind her ear, peeled the gum from its holding place, and popped the wad in her mouth. Quickly I left the kitchen and wondered how many rounds of chewing and ear storage that gum had been through. For someone who was accused of always wanting more by my grand-father, she sure was frugal, even with modest treats.

In the privacy of our home, where a strong pot of coffee was always brewing, Grandma Lily would let down her pious guard of trying to religiously follow dietary rules, and sipped a cup of forbidden coffee with my mother. Sometimes when my mother came to pour a refill, she would regain a semblance of restraint and say, "Just a schmid-geon. Oh, and while you are at it, would you pour in some water with the coffee?" Perhaps the water was to dilute her caffeine sins.

To pay mom back for the numerous hairdos, baths, and secret cups of coffee, Grandma Lily agreed to baby-sit my brother Bud. This arrangement was hatched by mom with the idea that supervising Bud's obsession with moving vehicles was essential if he was going to live to be potty trained.

Bud had a fondness for lying down in the middle of the main road that ran in front of our house. He raced up to the highway and plopped down right on the yellow line. His eyes closed as he enjoyed the warmth from the sun baked asphalt seeping through his clothes, that is, if he had any on that day. He arced his hands into a circle like he did for making snow angels so that he could feel the stark contrast of the rough texture of the asphalt and smoothness of the yellow line that divided the lanes. Another fun game was to roll his body off the highway as a car came by and then roll back on to the middle line after the car drove past.

Mom was playing Bingo in town at some school benefit and called home to see how things were going. "Bud was caught lying on the highway again, three times!" Celie sighed loudly in exasperation into the phone. When mom got home and criticized Celie for not supervising her little brother's activity, she defended herself, "Well, Lisa was supposed to watch him." Lisa looked up from her homework and said, "Kristy was supposed to watch him." Kristy was nowhere to be found. Bud was much faster than he looked capable of with the blubbery roll of baby fat that concentrated in his midsection. Whoosh, in a second he would be right up on the highway again.

Mother decided she needed to get a babysitter for the babysitters.

Hence, Grandma Lily came up to our house to keep Bud under house arrest while mom went to town to run some errands. My mother's last words as she went out the door were, "Keep Bud inside at all times no matter what. He is absolutely forbidden to go outside. Not matter how much he begs, he cannot go in the post yard." In spite of Grandma Lily's supervision and sole purpose to keep the little boy indoors, the day was very eventful. Twice Bud was brought up to the house by a post yard worker, rescued from his dangerous fixation on the treads on a giant tractor tire, oblivious that the tire was inches away from backing over him.

A neighbor lady brought Bud home two times, when he was caught playing with ornery cows that would have liked to sharpen their horns on him. Another time Bud was hauled back home when yet another neighbor rescued him from being imprisoned in an abandoned trailer wheel in a field where he had been pinned for a couple of hours. No telling how long he'd have been there if the neighbor hadn't been home and heard him crying.

My mother couldn't figure out how Bud got out so many times given that the door handles were higher than he could reach. It remains a mystery how he continued to escape since Grandma Lily was the only one home and only one who could open the door. Her brilliance in the matter was that when you aren't good at something, you aren't asked to do it again. Fortunate for her, she was off the hook for future babysitting.

My lucky day was when Grandma Lily asked me, "Honey, would you get a bath ready for me?" This was exciting to be the Chosen Helper. Immediately I stopped what I was doing, ran down the hall, and flung open the sliding door to complete my mission before someone else tried to take over this special job from me.

I turned both the hot and cold faucets full blast and ran my hand under the gushing water to make sure the temperature was just right. Grandma Lilly's rotund form hovered in the doorway to inspect the situation, teetering from one leg to another to shift the load. Her legs were thin at the ankles and curved into delicate calves and shapely thighs. From a distance, she looked like a ball on top of two shapely tooth picks.

As the water reached only about one and a half inches deep in the bath tub she said, "Okay, honey. That is enough water." Reluctantly I turned the water valves off and remained skeptical that she could possibly be correct in her assessment of the situation, even if she was an adult. Small birds need more water than that when they take a bath.

Slowly my grandmother lowered her bulky body into the tub. At the same time the water magically rose to the brim, close to overflowing. She leaned back and rested her head and let out a big sigh as she luxuriated in her bath with barely enough water to wet the feathers of a bird. I kept shaking my head, stunned and perplexed, trying hard to make sense of my grandmother's effect on liquids. This was my first science lesson in displacement, when her substantial post child-bearing body filled the tub and forced the water to evacuate and relocate to the brim.

Relaxing in her bath of just right water, Grandma Lily slumped down to have as much of that displaced water float on top of her as possible. Within minutes all those facial twitches melted away. Her eyes opened and closed gently, the eyebrows stayed in one place, and her mouth rested in a calm Mona Lisa smile. Her whole face went placid like a still lake, where not one fish was jumping. During those baths she was weightless, calm, and totally satisfied.

I don't recall if she ever told me she loved me. It is possible her love got used up from having all of those children. I never knew her deepest desires and unfulfilled wishes, although I have a feeling there were many. How is it that we can spend a lot of time with someone and not know them? There is one thing I do know. Grandma Lily loved her baths. The white bath tub surrounded her body like a cocoon and the water suspended the weight of her spirit so that she could be transported to a place where she was free of guilt, judgment, and twitches. This transcendent vision remains etched into my soul.

LISA DID THINGS DIFFERENTLY

BOREDOM, THAT EMPTY SPACE between interesting events, can either bring out one's creative spirit or motivate people to do bizarre things, especially in our rural neighborhood where we had to invent our own fun. However, if you are bored and nearly blind, like Lisa, sister number four in the pecking order, then adventure seeking could take some unusual twists in order to turn the ordinary into something new and interesting.

Starting out her young life with cataracts -a sporadic trend running through the family – Lisa saw the world as a black and white movie, because a white film covered her retina, like clouds masking the sun. This condition set her apart from her peers, especially from me, her twin, who had 20/20 eyesight with peripheral vision and a world that had color. Now the oldest sister Celie would have a rival over disabilities, over whose eyesight was worse. At the tender age of six, Lisa had to have a needle stuck in her eyeballs to remove the film. After cataract surgery, she came home wearing coke bottle glasses that made her grey eyes look like large owl orbs. As she blinked behind her thick lenses, every expression of hers was magnified. When she smiled, Lisa's face sparkled and glowed with her enthusiasm. When she scowled, dark brooding storm clouds formed and cast a gloomy shadow around her. "What is the matter? Did I say something wrong? Are you mad?" people would ask. My twin sister didn't have the words yet to say, "I'm just concentrating hard on seeing." Another aspect of being limited to straight forward vision is that something existed and, therefore, only mattered to Lisa if it was located right in front of her.

Her black glasses sat heavily on her small face. The thick lenses magnified everything so much that she couldn't get the whole picture of what she looked at. Lisa could see the letters but not the words. No matter how hard she focused, Lisa wasn't able to make out the details up close nor far away. Well, at least her world was now in color.

Looking into her eyes it was as if I could see deep into her soul. Peering closer into the grey space, I sensed a galaxy in there with orbits moving in their own mysterious ways. There were telltale signs of subtle rumblings of things going on inside of Lisa, mostly expressed in nonverbal kinds of ways. The tilt of her head, a concerned look, silent tears, quiet laughter. If people wanted to know what was going on in there, they had to really pay attention. Maybe Lisa's nonverbal manner was an understanding that words are inadequate and flimsy communicators for inward experiences.

Lisa was almost sister number three, except that I, being her much smaller twin and expected to be born last, elbowed her out of the way, swam toward the entrance to the world, and was born five minutes earlier. Lisa, being the larger twin and the one who should have been born first, had some things to say to me about this. "I think you took all the good stuff," she said. "You got the good eyesight, the skin that doesn't scorch in the sun, and social skills. Me, I just got the leftovers, the cataracts, and a red headed complexion that sunburns in five minutes. Plus, I don't know how to talk to people, especially groups of people. How do you do that?"

Despite the fact that we were opposites, a large part of being born five minutes apart is that we had to bear the burden of being compared. There seemed to be some confusion whether we were one or two individuals. "Oh, I see where one is plump and the other is skinny as a rail. How is that possible?" "Lisa, why aren't you more social, like Gina?" "Gina, why don't you study more like Lisa in school?" There was no getting around it. We were defined by the other. The more she had of something, the less I had of it. What I was, she was not. People scratched their heads in confusion as if they were trying to understand something that was out of their mental grasp, as they said, "One thing is for sure. You two sure are different."

At the home front, during visits from the neighbors, I would interrupt adult conversations, worm my way in to sit on laps, and then run off to find a more interesting activity. Lisa, on the other hand, would hang around the adults without needing to be a part of the conversation and be content to rock vigorously in her chair. In short, Lisa was a head banger.

Rocking her upper body back and forth in a chair, Lisa banged her head against the headrest, swaying back and forth, back and forth, rhythmically for hours, absorbed in her own internal world where time was meaningless. All the while, she stared straight ahead, holding a steady unblinking and unfocused gaze. Where did she go? Where she went no one knew. Hours later when the neighbors were going home she would still be rocking. Her blank face contained no hint of what might be going on inside.

One day Lisa was restless. Even though there were five horses to choose from to ride, or her bicycle with fancy fenders, light, and horn, not to mention crafty projects to paint and glue, Lisa still felt there was nothing to do. She had entered into that empty space, the void where the only thing that existed was is a sinking feeling that nothing was fun, and there would never be anything fun to do--ever again. Lisa took a deep sigh and said,

"I'm bored."

"Only boring people get bored,'" Mom said. "If you are bored, I'll give you something to do. There are dishes to be washed."

Quickly leaving the house and the chores that my mother was more than eager to delegate, Lisa went where she usually did when she needed to invent her fun. She crossed the highway in front of our home, crawled through the wooden gate of the horse pasture, and strolled up the hill to study the humongous ant pile that occupied the side of the horse trail. Any time the empty space where nothing was fun started to creep back in again, it was time to visit her friends, the ants, and figure out what they were up to and why.

Hundreds of frenetic red soldiers scurried around while a few carried a black beetle. Lisa's thoughts considered all aspects of ant living. The beetle's bulbous body looked like a burden too heavy to bear. Yet it was probably this year's ration of food. The red soldiers advanced millimeter by millimeter, up the steep grade of the mound.

Then the beetle was dropped and the carcass rolled back down, undoing hours of labor. Supposing that all things must have meaning, Lisa wondered if perhaps some of the ants lost their footing. One of them may have been clumsy. Maybe some of them weren't carrying their fair share of the weight. Mesmerized, Lisa spent the afternoon watching how these tiny creatures scrambled back under the hefty load and remained committed to their goal of getting that beetle into the hole at the top of the mound and stored in one of their food chambers.

On other excursions to the ant pile, Lisa would bend down close to the ground to follow the narrow trail of ants, trying to figure out their comings and goings, frowning when their trail disappeared underground. In other areas the narrow line of order became a patch of crazy activity with no direction to follow.

Watching them seemingly come out of nowhere and in a hurry to go somewhere, she thought to herself, "They must be doing something very important. How did they all know where to go? Where did their sense of belonging and working together come from?" These questions kept her coming back to the ant pile searching for answers.

The ants were so small and there were so many. Individually, each one could be dismissed as insignificant, a little like being one of many children. Yet, Lisa wanted to believe that each ant was important and worthy of further study.

Soon Lisa and I would find other activities that would make boredom disappear entirely. After reluctantly finishing our chores, we were on our own for finding entertainment. Preferably the faster and more dangerous the activity, the more fun it was. As soon as our feet were able to reach the gas pedal, we became qualified for driving the four wheel drive pickup truck.

Once we mastered the gas pedal, clutch, brakes, and gears by tearing around in horse pastures, we used the gravel road that circled our father's post and pole yard as a race track. We stomped on the gas pedal with our little feet for sudden acceleration. Then we pumped the brakes so hard that the tires screeched and skidded, the pickup fishtailing out of control. With enough build up of speed, the truck swerved around corners, barely regaining stability before veering around the next. This extreme sport, driven by nine year olds barely tall enough to see above the steering wheel, was motivated by seeing who could create the biggest dust storm.

Even though Lisa's vision made it difficult to even walk up and down stairs without becoming woozy, when it came to driving, she fearlessly took to the wheel. However, Lisa's approach was different. She drove as fast as she could, only backwards. As the passenger, I watched Lisa confidently yank the gear shift into reverse. Then she twisted her body and craned her neck so that she could look in the rear window behind her.

The tires tore into the gravel as she skidded around the corners and then stomped on the gas pedal to gather speed on the long stretches. Round and round and round she went- in reverse. After awhile, this became annoying for me as the passenger, to look ahead and see us retreating in fast motion, not knowing where we were headed.

"Why do you go backwards? Doesn't your neck hurt after an hour?" I asked, truly perplexed. I also wondered if she was a little on the crazy side and I needed confirmation one way or another.

"Because it's different," she said in a matter of fact manner, blinking for a few moments as she considered her answer. I couldn't argue with that.

While I remained skinny and scrawny, like a spindly weed, Lisa sprouted up and up and bloomed into a towering five foot ten inch babe with long flowing red hair. This growth spurt earned her the name "Big Red" in high school. Her glasses were replaced with contact lenses which provided a wide angle view of the world, visually and socially. Then, things changed in the boy department. For Lisa, however, boy chasing amounted to picking up hitch hikers.

The first hitchhiker was a five foot two inch red head with muscular broad shoulders, wearing no shirt. He thumbed a ride to work every day. Dad also happened to be his boss. Lisa's destiny changed the moment she stopped her car and the hitchhiker opened the door and slid onto the seat. His green eyes gazed up and down to check out her tall stature. His head nodded as if he was agreeing to an internal assessment. She would do just fine. Just fine. "Hey, about time you picked me up after all the times you've driven past," he said.

Lisa's eyes looked away and then she stole a look at him and turned away to hide her growing smile, noticing that his voice was pleasant to listen to. Velvety. Playful teasing, combined with a silky voice, was his winning formula for getting Lisa to conceive his child and marry him, in that order. All this while in her senior year in high school. The only complications were that the hitchhiker was already legally married to someone else, was posted as AWOL from the Coast Guard, had an alias name in which to keep under the radar screen with the law, and a tendency to walk around naked at parties. Instead of streaking, he slowly "snailed" through the crowd nude while making small talk along the way. While any of these issues would have created major obstacles for many people, they didn't seem to be a problem for Lisa.

Early in her pregnancy, she went into the principal's office one day and requested to take a couple of home studies so that she could graduate early. "Why do you want to graduate early?" the principal asked.

"It is what I want to do, and it is important that I do it," Lisa replied.

"We don't do home studies. Socializing is an important part of school. Kids are trying to grow up too fast these days," the principal said. He swiveled his chair back to his desk and shuffled through his papers. The secretary stapled papers and answered the ringing phone with her back to Lisa.

"I'm pregnant," she blurted. The secretary dropped the stapler and cleared the room. The principal rolled his chair in her direction and got out his pen.

"When do you want to start your home studies?" he asked.

Months later during a college preparation class, an instructor from the college system who was speaking to the high school asked if anyone had a disability in which that they might qualify for a grant. "Does being pregnant count as a disability?" Lisa asked loudly, visibly full and round with child.

A few years later, the marriage that was never legal in the first place, was annulled due to the hitchhiker's behavior going too far, even for Lisa's willingness to be flexible around his free spirit. He was rarely home unless he needed money or a place to sleep, so he wasn't missed much. Apparently hitchhiking was in his blood.

A few years later, Lisa was single and looking for a good man and so she picked up another hitchhiker. For many of my sisters, the motto was, "A good way to get over a man is to find someone new." Lisa saw him with his thumb out, standing on the side of the country road. She pulled over and rolled down the window. "Where are you going?" she asked.

"Wyoming," he said.

"But Wyoming is in the other direction," Lisa pointed out, trying to be helpful.

"I guess I am taking the scenic route," he said. She gestured for him to get in. The second that door opened and he slid in, Lisa's life was forever altered again. "I am hitchhiking because I sold my motorcycle for a pack of cigarettes since I didn't have enough money for gas," he said.

After a three hour conversation, a world record for this quiet hitchhiker, as he normally kept to himself, they cemented their relationship and started living together. A year later, Lisa got hitched to the second hitchhiker.

One day, Lisa's very honest six year old abruptly informed me while I was driving him somewhere, "My Mom doesn't pick up hitchhikers anymore."

About ten miles further down the road, he asked, "Are we going to run out of gas?"

"No, we aren't. See, look at all the gas in my tank," I assured him as we continued to drive down the road.

"My mom says only boring people get bored. Is that true?"

"That is what I've been told."

"What is boredom?"

"Well, it is an empty feeling that can come on so strong that it feels uncomfortable to be in our own skin, and nothing, I mean nothing, seems interesting. Minutes can seem like hours."

"How do you deal with it?"

"Well, it's like when you stub your toe. If you focus on how much the throbbing hurts, it only throbs more. So, the trick is to put your mind on other things and then your toe stops hurting. The thing is just to keep moving. Move your body. Move your mind. Reach for something else to think about or to do. The reaching for something positive is critical. And then, something will happen and you will feel like you can have fun again. Or, when you are old enough, you can drive backwards like your mother. It worked for her."

SORDID STORIES OF AN ORDINARY FAMILY

KRISTY IS THE MARRYING KIND

PART OF GROWING UP and thinking about events that shape our lives is wondering, "What if?" What if one thing had been different, how would that have changed the outcome? What if the right piece of advice came at the right time for Kristy, sister number five? How would things have turned out for her if my parents knew she wasn't really serious about getting married, and that she was just trying to get them riled? What would have happened if Dad had come to his senses, or Mom had put her foot down, or Kristy had decided to say what she really wanted before stepping up to the alter?

Kristy's claim to fame is that she said, "I do", to six marriages starting when she was fifteen. She then said, 'I want a divorce', six times as well. Once when I felt badly about missing a wedding,

I said to myself, "Oh well. I'll make sure I make it to the next one." That sweet smile and charm of Kristy's has attracted many eager suitors into her life, creating all sorts of unexpected dips and turns for her. Sometimes our strengths turned up too high can turn into our weaknesses. In Kristy's case, even charm has proven to have its downsides.

As a child, Kristy had ambitions of making money, like most kids who ran lemonade stands or sold common rocks. Her distinction, however, was that she really knew how to play to her strengths. While knocking on all the doors in the neighborhood with one hand, Kristy's other hand clutched shriveled carrots sticks that could be bent in two without breaking. When the neighbors' doors opened, she proudly held out the bounty that was for sale. With her sweet angelic round blue-green eyes, Kristy looked up into each potential customer's face, smiling widely in anticipation of a reward. Her lisp only added to her appeal. "Would you like to buy thome carrothhs?" The air escaped over the sides of her lazy tongue as she slurred and hissed through her sales speech. "Sthee thezzzzze carroths here. I can get thome more too."

Gazing down at Kristy's hopeful face, one neighbor lady never looked away or broke contact. It was as if the little girl must have come down from heaven. "Well, what have we here?" the neighbor lady cooed. She examined the wilted carrots as if they were precious cargo and called for her husband. "Honey, would you get the coin jar for me?" Ka-ching. Ka-ching. Along with her excitement over the fact that all her wilted "carrotths" were purchased by enthusiastic buyers, Kristy came home with pockets full of money and both hands tightly cupping more coins in her hands. She used the same wide-eyed and innocent look for getting out of reach of the paddling stick with Mom and Dad. One day I was outside in the yard collecting duck eggs to complete the necessary ingredients for my bread recipe. Since duck eggs have such large yolks, I only needed one duck egg for every two chicken eggs. An added bonus was that the bright orange yolk added a wild gamey flavor so mysterious that none of the dinner guests could guess what would make ordinary white bread taste so unusual. While I was hunched over collecting eggs hidden in clumps of tall grass in the yard, Kristy scurried around inside the house and locked every door. Then she stood waiting as the seconds ticked by, wondering what would happen once I realized who was in control of the situation now.

Kristy's smile grew wider and wider as she watched me jiggling the door handles, becoming more and more agitated. As I furtively ran from one locked door to another and glared into the windows, Kristy smiled back at me. My nostrils flared as I sniffed for blood, thinking of what I would do once I got a hold of a limb. BLAM! Glass shattered on the floor as my fist made contact. Then my hand reached through the broken window and unlocked the door. Now, standing in the doorway, I looked for my prey.

With the deft moves of a professional assassin, Kristy's hand opened a kitchen drawer and drew out a chef's cutting knife while her eyes stayed on me, following my every move. The blade glinted as she jabbed it toward my chest, letting me know she was serious and ready to commit injury, or murder if necessary to protect herself.

Quickly she put the knife back into the drawer. Then I became aware of the sound of Mom's pounding footsteps in the hall. "Okay," Mom demanded, "which one of you broke the glass window??!!" Mom looked at me and noticed the she-devil-on-fire look on my face. Kristy conjured up her sweet smile, with those pudgy gopher cheeks and teensy nose that was more of an afterthought. Who was Mother to suspect as the culprit? The she-devil or the angel with gopher cheeks? At that point, I knew I would be sacrificed to the paddling stick while she kept up her innocent appearances.

Even though Kristy's smile and charm often worked in her favor, they would lead her to all sorts of thorny entanglements with more at stake than a broken window. A few years later, at the ripe age of fifteen, Kristy asked Mom and Dad in her high pitched whispery voice, "What would you think if I wanted to get married to my boyfriend, who iszzth eighteen now, before I graduate from high szzzthchool?"

"Well," Mom sighed heavily, "it's not a good idea at your age. She sat down wearily and folded her hands in her lap and added, "But, I guess there is nothing we can do to stop you from getting married if that is what you really want...."

"This isn't like Mom to give up so easily," Kristy thought. "Where was her fire to crack the whip on ridiculous propositions and ability to intimidate to keep unruly kids in line?" What Kristy did not know was that Mom's life was turning into smoking rubble and ruins, of which would later come to play a bigger part in our lives. My mother didn't have any more fight left in her.

"Well, I'd like to support you in this if this is what you really want," Dad said as he leaned forward in his easy chair to pat Kristy's hand. Although Mom and Dad had dealt with the complexities of keeping up with a houseful of children, there was now no unified parental front for these kinds of adolescent hassles, particularly children wanting to marry.

"Doesn't anyone know this conversation about getting married was not supposed to make it past your strong objections and outright 'NO'? It was only intended to get you riled. Why aren't you protesting?" All of these things she thought to herself.

The marriage conversation would probably have withered and died a natural death, but was revived a few months later by Dad. Kristy and her boyfriend were visiting in the living room when Dad asked, "Hey, do you two still want to get married?" Not knowing if her boyfriend was really serious about this far fetched concept or not, Kristy sat back and watched the conversation unfold.

"Sure, we want to get married," her boyfriend declared, leaning forward on the edge of the couch to show his earnest desire.

Dad got up from his favorite olive green easy chair that sagged in the seat cushion from many hours of contemplating finances, kids, his own marriage, and now, marrying the young. In a fatherly fashion, he put his arm around the boyfriend's back. He asked in his booming voice that made questions sound like demands, "Hey, how about we two take a walk to have a word?" Their heads leaned toward each other as if they were privately hatching a conspiracy. They strolled off to speak man-to- man about marriage and who knows what else.

After a short while, Dad and the boyfriend sauntered back to Kristy with the conclusion of their whisperings. "Okay, it's a done deal. You're gonna get married." Dad said as his face beamed with a wide smile. My father never spoke to Kristy about her concerns around the marriage. Apparently, it was sufficient to have the conversation between the guys.

Kristy sucked in her breath. Having never thought it would have come to this point, she was now on new uncharted terrain where you skip the growing up part and go straight to marriage. Dad's chest swelled with pride as he declared, "Whatever dress you want, you can get. Get as many flowers as you want. The photographer- the more pictures the better. Let me know how many bride's maids dresses you want and how many groomsmen there will be. WHATEVER YOU WANT." Where the money would come from was unclear but not a deterrent for my father. This marriage was going to happen come hell or high water. And Dad's determination would be tested.

Two nights before the big event, Kristy was driving late at night from a nearby town and stopped at her boyfriend's mobile home. She knocked on the door of the place that was soon to be her new home in a few days and opened it. She heard a scurrying sound. Her boyfriend had his shirt open and was zipping his pants as he was coming toward the door. "What isth going on here?" she demanded. She looked in the bedroom, scanned the rumpled sheets, and smelled trouble in the air.

A few long strides later, she was scoping out the bathroom and found a naked woman cowering behind the shower curtain. "I sttthould cancel the wedding," said Kristy. "No, you know you won't," the boyfriend said. She thought of her father's efforts at making sure this wedding would happen and the money he was dumping into it. Her boyfriend was right. She was going to go through with it, despite her murderous impulse to behead him on the spot.

One day before the wedding, the priest called Dad to inform him that his daughter was too young to be married by law, even with parental consent. Since she wasn't pregnant, the law would forbid a marriage of a girl under sixteen. Kristy sighed with relief. She thought she was off the hook. Not to be deterred, however, that very same day, Dad flew Kristy, the boyfriend, and himself to Salt Lake City, where they marry the very young. The pressure was on again.

"Time to suck it up and smile through the ordeal," she thought to herself, resigning herself to her fate. The next day they flew back just in time to go through the scheduled performance of getting married in front of one hundred and fifty friends and family.

The local ceremony went off without any further complications. No one knew they had already been married just hours ago, so it seemed like the real deal. As I listened to the ceremony, I heard Kristy say with her breathy voice of a child, "I promith to honor and obey. I do take thisth man asth my husthband. Til death do uth part." As she stood at the alter, I could see the little girl was still in her, the charming one who sold carrots at rip-off prices and had people thank her for the opportunity.

I stared at the six groomsmen who wore canary yellow tuxedos and the six bridesmaids in their full length yellow ruffled dresses, flanking the child bride and barely adult groom, looking like shiny sugar frosting decorations on the edge of a wedding cake.

After the ceremony, we all descended down to the church basement to eat the wedding cake. Following tradition, the top tier was put aside to store safely in the freezer for celebrating a successful first year of marriage. A few months later, however, the freezer with the cake was unplugged and put into storage when the marriage failed to last "until death do us part". Since no one now wanted anything to do with the cake, it thawed, grew green and black with mold and crumbled. Shortly thereafter, when I was helping Kristy move the freezer into her new house and new life, we came across the cake. Kristy shrugged at the round cake box like it had become an ancient relic of her past life that now seemed like a distant memory.

Although still a tender youth in years, Kristy could never go back to reclaim her innocence and more time for growing up free from adult concerns. Getting married became a one way door. Once she entered this grownup passageway, her childhood snapped shut behind her. Standing on the other side of the door, her eyes scanned the horizon looking for anything familiar. Not recognizing the landscape, she did what she did best: smile and look ahead.

"Even though my fairy tales have proven to be false, the view from here is still pretty good," she thought. Her hardships had cured her soul like a piece of leather. She was now durable, but supple and ready to create a positive future, many possible futures. Moving forward, Kristy's charms got her roped into getting married five more times- so far. Apparently, for her, it is important to remember, if at first you don't succeed, try, try, try, try, try, try again.

SORDID STORIES OF AN ORDINARY FAMILY

CAROL'S WILD CARNIVAL RIDE

"SORRY TO REPORT THAT you have an-other daughter," the doctor playfully teased Dad when Carol was born. It was no secret around our house that a son was increasingly hoped for with each arrival of another baby girl. Perhaps that is where Carol came up with the idea that she was the sixth mistake. Maybe this notion was what gave her permission to live life on the edge, in the fast lane, Janis Joplin style, and run off with the carnies. When needing guidance in her life, instead of wondering, "What would Jesus do at this moment?" Carol was more of the mind to ask "What would Janis do?" To Carol, freedom was just another word for nothing left to lose.

As a baby, Carol enjoyed celebrity status as people admired the contrast of her vibrant auburn hair against her creamy complexion and quiet nature. Then things changed. One day, a big chunk of hair was sawed off her bangs right to the scalp, marring her darling appearance. Mom yelled, "SOME VARMINT CUT CAROL'S HAIR! Which one of you did it?" All of us sisters shrugged our shoulders and looked confused. The culprit was never found.

Then another change occurred. This quiet darling found her voice. That was our code for she talked a lot. Carol rambled on and on and on allowing no space between sentences with a voice that blew like a fog horn down the road and through the neighborhood. She carried on her monologues until her listeners were numb from the overload of verbal stimulation and fell silent and unresponsive with fatigue. Her talkative personality was also part of her little girl charm, so she was not faulted for having a lot to say.

In addition to the sixth child adding to the chaos of all of us living under one small roof, Mom was always busy doing tons of laundry, unrelenting cleaning of muddy floors, and cooking food for the masses. Her other full time duty was to extend country hospitality and pots of coffee to truckers who transported my father's posts and poles, and the grimy work crew who tracked in mud from the post yard. Then there were relatives who dropped off their kids and frequent visits from neighbors who came at all hours and stayed all day. Turning someone away was often a fantasy but not considered an option. Hence, there was very little time left over for parental guidance.

Guidance, according to Carol's memory, amounted to strict orders by Mom to "BE BACK BY DINNER." It wasn't "get good grades, brush your teeth, clean your room, be nice to your sisters, obey your parents, be a good girl, or think about what you want to be when you grow up and plan for it." Anyway, memory is selective and keeping track of mealtime was the only requirement that stuck in Carol's mind.

Mealtime usually included our growing family, some of our friends, as well as frequent adult guests all squished in around the crowded table. One night at dinner, Carol was picking on a guest by jabbing her fork into his ribs to get him to move over a few inches so she could have some elbow room. Mom said, "You cut that out or I'll give you a jab so you know how it feels."

Carol's mouth puckered and turned down. Mom warned her, "Don't cry or I will give you something to cry about." In Carol's efforts at holding back a big sob, she dropped her spoon in her dessert and the whipped cream splattered in her eye. We laughed in unison at her comical sight. Now her whole face puckered.

"Dummy, dummy," Carol muttered under her breath, barely audible but with a hiss of venom behind it.

"WHAT did you say?" Mom asked, in her deep baritone voice she used for intimidation and extracting confessions.

"I said my brother is handsome," Carol replied

loud enough for everyone to hear, as her head hung down to her collarbone.

Carol's green eyes smoldered like hot coals as she finished dinner and skipped desert. The next morning Mom saw her headed out the front door with yesterday's pigtails still in place. Her black tights had a hole in the knee and sagged at the ankles. Her coat sleeves hung past her fingers. Both of her shoes were for two right feet.

"And just where do you think you are going?" Carol looked down to her shoes. "Are you running away?" Mom asked.

Nodding her head up and down, Carol retorted, "I'm runnin' away and no one is gonna to stop me."

"What do you have in your suitcase?" Mom asked. Carol opened up her suitcase which included most of her clothes, snow boots, and a plastic pistol.

"We would be terribly lonesome without you." Mom said. Carol stared out the front door waiting for this conversation to end so she could be on her way. "If you left, we would have to get another girl to take your place," Mom said.

Carol hung her head down, admitting defeat, and dropped her suitcase. She never said another word about running away-- until years later. By then she would mean it and no one would be able to talk her into staying because she wouldn't care who took her place.

One evening Mom prepared a meal of tender roast and potatoes she had baked most of the day, complimented by warm homemade bread, and freshly picked green beans. The green bean plate was passed to Carol. Carol passed it on to the next person. Mom glanced over to Carol's plate and noticed the missing green beans. Prodding her to do the right thing, Mom said, "Eat those green beans. They will put hair on your chest!" I guess my mother was trying to convey they were good for you in a round-about way.

Carol's mouth grimaced. The grimace spread to her whole face as her eyes squeezed shut. Then in anguish she cried, "BUT I DON'T WANT HAIR ON MY CHEST!" She gulped for air and blurted, "I WANT IT IN MY ARMPITS!" Carol was inconsolable and refused to eat her green beans that night. With visions of our own hairy chests looming in the future, the rest of us sisters pushed our portion of the now creepy green vegetable to the side of our plates.

As Carol's restless spirit began to develop she entertained herself with things that moved fast. One day she secretly hopped on her bicycle and sped off in haste before anyone could ask her to do the dishes or mop the floor. Her goal was to bicycle as fast as she could down a bumpy grassy slope called the "Forbidden Hill" by Mom. Carol pedaled to the peak, looked down the steep slope and noticed the path took a strong left turn at the bottom. The thought crossed her mind that if she didn't make the sharp turn, that asphalt, rocks, and gravel lay straight ahead.

Carol straightened up and positioned her pedals high so she could bear her weight down for maximum acceleration. Whoosh! Her shoulders shook from the jolts from riding the bumps as she rapidly descended. One more bump to go. Then both wheels went airborne. Wind blurred her vision.

The next thing Carol remembered was her face jammed into the asphalt. Lifting her head, Carol groaned as her body registered the impact of rocks and asphalt on skin. Standing, she lifted her arms up to see if they still worked and noticed newly emerging purple areas around the elbows that felt like burning bonfires. Her eyes, flinching from the pain, inspected the little rocks embedded into the deep gashes of her bleeding flesh. She moved her legs to check if she could walk. Blood trickled from her shredded knee caps. Looking around, Carol located her bicycle a hundred feet away. With all the energy she could muster, Carol staggered and limped over to the bike and slowly pedaled home.

When she hobbled into the house, Mom noticed her puffy lips and bruised face and asked her to open her mouth. Just as she had suspected but hoped it wasn't true. Carol's front tooth had broken off almost to the gum line.

After the swelling around her mouth went down, the dentist gave Carol a silver tooth until a new porcelain replacement arrived. During this time we referred to her as Tinsel Tooth. Once she had a full set of teeth again, Carol resumed her fast moving life.

Her dare-devil lifestyle, however, almost stopped one day when Carol proved that babysitting could be dangerous, if not deadly. When she was thirteen she found herself watching over a boy almost the same age as her, as well as a younger girl and a toddler. Even though the boy was twelve and the legal age to be by himself, his parents felt he needed a babysitter. They said, "He's slow."

Carol was having a hard time connecting with the boy. All the children looked at her with boredom, stared at the clock, and counted the minutes until mommy and daddy got home. "Watching the sun go across the sky in slow motion is better than this dingy living room," Carol thought as she took the children outside to the back yard. She scanned the blue sky in hopes that the sunshine would rescue this gloomy situation. "So, how is school going?" Carol asked. The boy avoided eye contact and turned away from her without answering. He hadn't learned how to fake it in life and hide his awkward feelings.

They watched an orange cat claw its way up a pole and hang out on the power line. Seconds later, the cat went rigid and fell to the ground with its blank yellow eyes wide open. Without anyone saying anything about the electrocution incident, Carol guided the children indoors to get away from the death scene.

"Does anyone want to play cards?" Carol asked.

"No," they murmured, as they looked down at their hands.

Then the subject of guns came up. The boy looked into Carol's eyes and smiled and wind milled his arms around in excitement. He said, "My Grandpa has a GUN and it's gonna be MINE someday. Wanna see it?"

"Bulls eye! We have established COMMON GROUND," Carol thought. After all, she was a bit of a dead eye herself in regards to gunmanship.

The boy ran out of the room and into the den. He opened up the gun cabinet and snatched the 270 Power Rifle out of the wooden rack. Just as Carol walked into the den to see what he was up to, he pulled the rifle out of its leather pouch.

In her mind, everything moved in slow motion. She put her hands up in protest and said, "Noooooo, dooooonnn'tttt dooooo thaaaattttt." At the same time her eyes saw the boy's finger hit the trigger as he clumsily pulled the rifle out of its leather casing. Boom! Crack! Carol didn't feel a thing. However, she figured that the blood flowing from her neck meant she had been hit.

She put her hands on the backs of the children and escorted them to the living room and said, "Stay here until I say you can move. Okay?" With her mind going blank, she picked up the phone and called the hospital without knowing the number or using a phone book. Maybe divine intervention put the call in. Carol's mind went dark and she felt her legs buckle from underneath her. The paramedics rushed through the door minutes later and found the children sitting in the living room, just as they were told to do. Carol was lying in the kitchen on the floor in a pool of blood with the phone in her hand.

The losses were high. The bullet went through her right shoulder, shattered her collarbone and tore off part of Carol's right nostril. A bruised lung filled up with fluid and shrapnel peppered the insides of her body. Her favorite crème colored cowboy boots with snake skin tips were ruined from laying in the pool of blood. Even the local paper announced her as dead. The boy's parents told him that he killed her. This was to teach him a lesson about safety and the proper handling of guns. Also, it was Friday the thirteenth.

During the three weeks in intensive care, Carol gradually inched away from death and moved toward fulfilling the possibility of living to adulthood. Somewhere in her mind she heard a conversation, "but it was an unloaded gun". The nurses found their purpose by doting on Carol's every need. For three weeks, they cooed at her simply being able to blink an eye upon waking, and showed their approved when she was able to sit up in bed without assistance. After watching her inch closer to becoming stronger and more self sufficient, all the nurses became teary eyed when their source of joy and inspiration left the hospital. Bonding through adversity. Life went back to normal and perhaps became a little duller. And then all hell broke lose.

The carnival, with its lights, games, and exciting rides, came to town for three days in the summer. For Carol, restless and oozing with estrogen, the carnival was the highlight of the whole year. She and her friends charmed the carnies into giving them free rides by flashing smiles and sweeping their long hair out of their faces to make brief eye contact. Free rides turned into extra long rides. Carol swooshed up and down in the Silver Bullet. The swings on the ride called the Cage went round and round, lifting higher and higher until her mouth was involuntarily pried open from the centrifugal force and Carol's head was pinned against the cage. The blur of images as she went round and round and living for the moment in fast motion was just the drug Carol was looking for. As long as she stayed on those two rides, life was F-U-N.

The carnie running the Silver Bullet smiled big and wide as soon as Carol was in the line. He stared at her long red hair and the possibilities that might come with it. She felt their chemistry sizzle as he gazed at her and she gazed back. He guided her into the wire cage. He slammed the door, locked it, and said, "It's on the house, you sweet thing." She returned to the carnival everyday for three days looking for love at the Silver Bullet.

Then Carol and her friends came to watch the carnival close down. No more glowing lights, no more games with prizes and no more exhilarating rides taking her to ecstasy. The thought of not seeing the Silver Bullet man became unbearable. If he had to leave town, she had to go with him she decided. Her car was packed and her dog was sitting in the back seat as she prepared to join him on the next leg of the carnival journey.

In Carol's mind, this abrupt departure in the middle of the night without telling anyone wasn't running away. She was just leaving town to experience the world. Carol figured that since she was probably a mistake, she wouldn't be missed anyway. Besides, she didn't want to end up being a farmer's wife with leathery skin. Being a carnie's woman would at least involve some travel and adventure.

"My only condition for going with you is that I have to have a shower every day," Carol said to her carnie man.

"That might be tough to find traveling the way we do," he said.

"Well, the deal is, if you want me to go with you, then you need to promise me that you will find a shower every day for me." With hands on her hips, she declared, "Or I won't go."

"Okay, it will be hard to find a shower. But you have a deal. Let's get going," he said.

Around midnight on that night Carol decided it was better to be with a carnie than become a farmer's wife, Mom noticed that Carol had not returned home. "Gina," Mom said, "would you take my car and go into town and see if Carol is around? And once you find her, bring her right home."

I drove to teenage hangouts under lampposts on Main Street where someone could be seen by anyone looking for action. I rolled down the window and yelled, "Hey, have any of you seen Carol?" Their eyes were glazed and cigarettes hung from their adolescent lips. "No man, wow man, Carol, no haven't seen her," they mumbled, trying to convey excessive sincerity of caring. They looked like Future Criminals of America and probably wouldn't have told me anything anyway, but it was worth a try.

Feeling like a cop patrolling the hood, I cruised past bars and dark school yards, asking huddled groups of her peers if anyone had seen Carol. "When was the last time you saw her? I have something important to say to her." I pleaded with them, trying to motivate someone to snitch on her secret lair. "No man," they all murmured in union, "haven't seen her in days."

Giving up on my search I drove home to deliver the news, "Mom, I can't find her anywhere." I slumped into the couch and looked at the clock. It was close to 2:30 a.m. I noted, in case I had to fill out a police report. Mom sighed, put down the newspaper, and walked over to the phone to report a missing person to the sheriff's department.

A couple hundred miles away Carol started her new life of freedom. She watched the blinking bright lights attracting throngs of people, like moths flying toward the lights. Carol walked among the players on the midway trying their luck on games promising prizes. The thrilled screams from passengers in rides that scrambled your brains was proof she had entered into the world of the eternal party. While she was meeting new exotic people with tattoos, my mother and I lost sleep.

One day, Carol and her carnie man had a work

detail of driving a thirteen speed Road Ranger truck. Their job was to drive to a location down the road and pick up one of the rides and transport it to the next spot. In carnival lingo, they were "dead heading" with an empty load en route to pick up a load.

"Do you want to drive this monster?" he whispered in her ear.

"Get me into that driver's seat and I will take you where ever you want to go," she whispered back into his ear as she nuzzled his neck.

She slid into the driver's seat and proceeded to grind the gears. Her focus was so absorbed in figuring out how to shift that she wasn't watching the road or aware of the fact she was going only twenty five miles per hour. When she looked up, police lights were flashing. Carol promptly lurched the Road Ranger over to the side of the road.

The policeman poked his head in the car and sniffed the air. Carol leaned forward to turn the blaring music down. He started his investigation by asking, "Are you a runaway?"

"No I am not a runaway," Carol responded sincerely. After all, in her mind she just left town to explore the world. It wasn't the same thing as running away.

The officer narrowed his gaze and stared into her green eyes waiting for her to break down. Her eyes stayed locked into his and held steady. He shifted his eyes to look around, sniffed the air, and seemed disappointed. "Well," the policeman asked, "do you have a license to operate this vehicle?" He got her there on that technicality.

"No, I am just practicing." Carol responded.

The policeman spit his chew onto the side of the road and said as he backed away from the Road Ranger, "You just make sure he drives from here on out."

"Yes sir," said Carol and her carnie man in unison.

They continued their drive and picked up the load. On the way back into town the city cops were lying in wait on the side of the road. Apparently cousins once removed had seen Carol at the carnival and felt her presence was suspicious and turned her in. Mom and Lisa, the sister chosen for support this time, drove to the police station and picked her up. "What were you thinking?" Mom asked. "That no one would find you?" Carol stared at her mother while she contemplated the answer and said, "I didn't think anyone would miss me."

Lisa rode back with Carol and her dog in case she tried to defect. These concerns were realized, only six months later. Due to longings from being in love and suffering from long distance blues, Carol quit high school and joined up with her man and the carnival for the next season. Each carnival delivered exactly what she was looking for. Whoosh!!! Lifting up into the air in the Silver Bullet ride, turning over and over and over until she didn't know which way was up, achieving the euphoria of no rules, no boundaries, and time blurring with no set hours. Just freedom, with nothing to lose. Just for something novel to do,

Carol ran the mirror joint where winning dart throwers walked away with mirrors adorned with rock band emblems. Then, after a few days of being in one place, it was time for the carnival to move on, time for Carol to see a new place and meet new people.

Then life on the move came to a standstill when Carol's man hurt his hand while he was operating a ride. When his duties were reduced to unglamorous work away from the lights, rides, and games, there was no more magnetic attraction to the carnival life, so he up and quit. Carol and her man returned to ordinary "civilian" life and she got a job at a local hardware store where they sell "screws and shit".

One afternoon while we were hanging out by the lake, I asked Carol if she missed the freedom of life on the road. "Well," she said, "look what freedom did for my heroine Janis Joplin. She's dead now. I'm not so sure about what it means anymore. I used to think driving fast on a motorcycle with my hair blowing in the wind was freedom. But now I think of the knots I have to untangle afterwards. I guess I care about more things than I used to. Can you care about things and be free? While I was on the road in between carnival set ups, I picked up a kid's book and discovered something. Sometimes we need to make new rules, and Dr. Suess has the simple guideline all laid out. "It's fun to have fun, but you have to know how."

SORDID STORIES OF AN ORDINARY FAMILY

BUD HAS FRECKLES EVERYWHERE

WHEN MY BROTHER Bud entered the world as the youngest and only son in a family of six sisters- all of whom were soon to join the new order of feminists- a vortex of swirling estrogen and testosterone collided. Friends and neighbors chimed in unison, "That poor boy, being the youngest with all those sisters." Even Mom and Dad declared, "We had better keep our baby boy from harm." This protective stance seemed a little over reactive to me. Wasn't sibling rivalry the natural order of things, necessary for developing important social skills? Besides, Bud had some of his own strengths to play to in defending himself from us girls.

By the age of five, Bud had sprouted into a three foot high by almost three foot wide boy, with fiery red hair and alabaster white skin that burned easily and would eventually acquire lots of freckles. "That boy sure is stout," people marveled. My father marveled as well but for different reasons. Blinking in amazement, Dad observed his son walk past a pile of GI Joe soldiers in favor of playing with our dolls. Sitting on the floor, Bud nurtured the plastic babies with the sincerity of a new mother. "Wanna eat somethin'? Do you need to go poddy?" he cooed as he wedged one of them between his arm and pudgy chest.

Then, in the corner of the living room he spotted his missing dump truck. Switching his focus, Bud lifted the doll by the hair high into the air and flung it across the room where it skidded on the floor and crashed into the wall. As he stood up, Bud forgot about the truck for a moment and spontaneously swept his arms up above his head in a graceful arc. Round and round he turned on his hefty square feet, his eyes looking down at his footwork while his fingers reached for the ceiling.

Concern set further in Dad's face as he saw his only begotten son's strong and stocky body squirm and writhe as Bud expressed himself through whimsical body movements. He shimmied and gyrated while slithering up and down. As my mother watched him dance, she thought, "My son is becoming more handsome every day." Dad was thinking, "All this time waiting for a son and now he wants to play with dolls and dance. I wonder if I have a pansy for a boy." My father shook his head in confusion and went back to the post yard. There he knew where things stood. Hard work was easy to understand.

A moment later Bud closed his hand, turned to the nearest person, whoever it was, lowered his arms, and bonked the unsuspecting victim on the head with his heavy fist. Their eyes rolled and blinked in shock for a few moments as they recovered from the trauma. The next moment Bud's fists loosened, fingers opened up, and his arms gracefully arced over his head again and then lightly returned to his sides. His moves resembled a cross between a midget sumo wrestler and prima ballerina.

Even though Bud had thumped adults two or three times his size, Mom and Dad continued to shield this miniature heavy weight champion from being picked on. Whenever there was a squirmish that involved a sister and Bud, one of our parents would run into the room and demand confession, "Okay, which sister is guilty?" Clearly, if we were going to ambush the little darling, we had to make sure it was out of earshot.

Despite the superior cunning and advantages of maturity we older sisters possessed, Bud, even at the tender age of five, had a very effective way to overcome this power imbalance. He didn't plan an ambush, or trick us into yucky situations such as putting spiders in our food, grossing us out by eating a bug, or pushing worms in our face. We could have handled that. He possessed something we didn't- a penis. This gender equipment of his was a disruptive aberration to our female sensitivities to say the least.

Mom dressed him every morning. Every day he wiggled out of his clothes, tore them off, or somehow stepped out of them. Determined to have her baby boy properly dressed so that she would look like a good mother to the public, Mom forced them back onto his flailing arms and kicking feet. Despite her efforts, it was just a matter of minutes and his shirt slumped in the grass in the yard. Under the monkey bars his shoes were left to bake in the sun. Days later his pants would be rescued from the horse pasture. His underwear blew across the highway that ran past our house. On a hot day, it was amazing how the eighteen wheels of a semi truck pounded those briefs right into the asphalt. After several hundred attempts, my mother gave up on keeping Bud dressed, or even partially clothed. It seemed impossible to contain his untamed spirit by the social custom of clothes. Eventually this set the stage for Bud's getting even with us girls.

Being older, we were expected to help out in the affairs of the household, set the dinner table, and bring out the food. The only begotten son, due to his youth, got to play while we worked. Bud's only mealtime responsibility was to show up at the dinner table just as the food was being served. Steaming pots were placed on the table. Everyone sat down to eat. Bowls were passed around. With requests for salad dressing, pass me this, pass me that, and the clang of forks and knives scraping the plates, the din of large family dining began.

Bud was perched on his wooden high chair,

which he had outgrown a year ago, putting his torso at the same height as the table in full view should he exercise his male tendency for scratching his juvenile genitals, or gonads as they were known in our house. At some point, there was a clatter of a fork dropping on the plate and a sister cried out, "Ooooh! Bud! That is disgusting!" The rest of us looked in his direction and cried out, "OOOOH!" We whined as irritation set in, "I am trying to eat! Get some clothes on!!" Chaos broke out. Chairs screeched across the floor and doors slammed as we defiantly left the table until his body parts were covered.

Without lifting a finger- except to itch himself- Bud had the power to disrupt a whole dining experience, get his sisters to vacate the premises, cringe, and even weaken at the knees. He got us in the one spot where we were most vulnerable- a phobic aversion to the penis. As sisters, we rarely agreed on the same thing at the same time, but around this we were unified. "GET SOME CLOTHES ON, BUD!!"

Eventually, roaming the hillsides without clothes would have its consequences. In nature, every critter has a weakness that can bring it down, despite its mighty strength or its other capabilities. For some, a sense of curiosity can lure it into fatal situations. For others, poor eyesight can make them prey to the stealthy. Or they might trust the playful nature of a coyote and be cut down in the next minute. One of Bud's weaknesses was his skin's extreme sensitivity to sun exposure, which, coupled with his aversion to clothes made him particularly vulnerable to the outdoors. Within minutes of being in the sun, his skin scorched and burned, peeled, or freckled, or all of the above. More than once, Bud was spotted soaking in a cool bath to draw the heat from a second degree sun burn.

That poor tender white skin. It went from pasty pale without a trace of pigment to a series of burned blotches. Eventually, Bud developed a severe case of uneven skin pigmentation, otherwise known as massive freckles. On boring days we threatened to play the Connect the Dots game on him. Freckles popped up on his ears, way down into his ear canal, speckled his eyelids, and even formed constellations on his butt. The dots kept popping up until there were so many they started clustering into clumps, though not quite evenly enough to qualify as a tan. There were still a few open spaces that were susceptible to the sun's searing effects.

Privately, Bud worked behind the scenes in an effort to change his standing as the freckled joke. During bath time, in a futile attempt to rub off some of those dots, he vigorously scrubbed his skin with a bar of Lava soap, an abrasive hand cleaner with ingredients deigned to rub off hard to-remove gunk. If that didn't work soon, he was contemplating moving on to harsher abrasives. Bud was enticed by Comet's promise on its can that its powder coupled with the bleach would "remove even the toughest of stains!"

Eventually we tired of the freckle jokes and looked for other kinds of adventures to have with our baby brother. We became inspired to prey upon a weakness of Bud's. That was his innocence. His inexperience of not having been in the world very long and not knowing deceit made Bud gullible for scamming. Often in nature, the youngest, weakest, and most inexperienced are singled out for prey. Bud was a sure target amongst us wily sisters who had once been innocent ourselves.

"If you do the dishes Bud," Kristy said, "I will love you more than I already do. When it is your turn to do the dishes, I'll do them." Bud did the dishes, bathing in the idea of Kristy's attention and the payback. When the rotation of chores made Bud the dish washer, he said to Kristy, "It's your turn to do the dishes." Kristy said, "I never agreed to that. You must be crazy." She looked at her friend and said, "Let's ditch him," as they ran out of the house and galloped away on the horses.

Celie, whose clothes reeked because she had just been sprayed by a skunk said to Bud, "If you clean my shoes and pants, I will give you twenty five cents, but you need to get rid of the stink completely to get the money." Bud plugged his nose and stewed the tennis shoes and pants in boiling hot soapy water in the bucket outside in the cold night where the stench could be tolerated by the stars. He rinsed them with one hand while the other hand held his nose. When he presented them to Celie, she sniffed and said "They still stink. They need to be washed again." He soaped and rinsed them again, and presented his hard work to her again to her. She sniffed and said, "They still stink so I don't owe you any money. Sorry." He looked at his raw red hands and walked away.

To further exploit his innocence, I mentored Bud in the skill of lying. I figured someone had to break him into the concept of spoken untruths sooner or later and gladly assumed the role of teacher. "Bud, we do not have any more chocolate popsicles," I said. He contemplated this statement and looked into the freezer and saw the popsicles plain as day. "Yes we do," he said. I opened the freezer door, peered in, and then said, "No we don't," with complete conviction of a believer. Bud opened the freezer again and saw the frosty wrappers. His eyes rolled up as he whipped his head around from left to right and back again, confused with what he saw to be true and what he heard from a trusted source. Double fun for me. Two lessons in one--the bold faced lie and who can you trust. I weakened from a feeling of giddiness and laughter spilled out of me as I witnessed this precious moment of his simple view of the world of truth telling and trust colliding with my deceit.

There were other trials for the only son to endure as well. On days we drove to the city nearby to eat in a restaurant, Mom would ask, "Where do you want to eat? Pat's Diner or the Gold Mine? We sisters all shouted "Pat's Diner!" Our arms shot up in unison showing the vote. "Okay," Mom said, "how many for the Gold Mine?" "I do," Bud said, raising his solitary arm and solo voice repeating,

"I vote for the Gold Mine!" "Sorry," said Mom, "the majority has voted for Pat's Diner, so Pat's Diner it is." Bud looked down into his lap, tasting the bitterness of defeat. Again. Mom added, "The majority rules, Bud, and that is fair. It says so in our Constitution of the United States. That is an important part of our democracy."

"I don't like that rule," Bud said.

"If democracy and majority rule is good for the nation," Mom responded, "it must be good for the family."

"Then," Bud pouted, "I don't like democracy." Bud had no words for saying that he desired a form of democracy where the single voice counted for something.

Being a loner, which was forced upon him by his age and gender, Bud spent more and more of his play time hanging out at the post and pole yard, just a stone's throw from the home front. He transported piles of sawdust in the toy dump trucks from one end of the tractor shed to the other. Other days he filled his dump trucks with discarded remnants of wood pieces and moved them to a corner of the shed, stacking the wood scraps in long and high rows. Most of the time-being daddy's only little boy- Bud spent riding amongst the dirty chains in back of dad's seat on the tractor. This is where the guys got to practice solidarity.

Occasionally Dad stopped the tractor, shut down the motor, and turned around to his son. "Okay Bud, we are hauling forty bundles of post.

How many trips do we need to make if we have two bundles each trip?" Then my father started up the motor again and roared off to give Bud time to count. When Bud finished his adding and had used all of his fingers and toes to keep track of counting, he tapped Dad on the shoulder to indicate that he was ready to present the answer.

Bud started looking at the world in terms of adding, subtracting, dividing, and multiplying while helping Dad transport wood in the post yard to be cut, peeled, preserved and delivered. Pretty soon Bud wouldn't need his fingers and toes to keep track and he could keep ideas in his head. Over time, Bud's sumo wrestler build of three foot by three foot was growing taller and his legs were thick as tree stumps. He was turning into the kind of guy school coaches wanted to have on their football team.

Like the seasons, things change. Power can shift once we discover we have it, that we always had it in some way. Every creature is powerful when it discovers its strength. The tiny little gnat, when it buzzes around fulfilling its function, has the nuisance power to drive people crazy. The elephant too. You don't want to be in its path when it decides to move. Then there is everything in between, all powerful if we pay attention to our strengths.

I came to accept this lesson one day when I playfully yet forcefully walked into Bud to show my assumed dominance as the older sister. I had become accustomed to smiling at my victory as he fell backwards a few steps. He would quickly regain his balance and retain his calm demeanor. Indifference was his tactic for restoring his sense of power, like "Hey man, that was no big deal. So what?"

However, on this day, I rammed my body into his and ricocheted off Bud like a gnat that had been swatted away and flattened. Bud stood sturdy as an elephant and smiled back like a predator licks its chops as it contemplates its much weaker and disadvantaged prey. I knew then times had changed and that Bud wasn't going to be pushed around anymore by estrogen. Being the older sister no longer held clout.

Football practice drills turned Bud into muscle. However, at the same time, inside his mind a weakness still existed. He felt self conscious about how his flaming red hair and massive freckles set him different from others. He still quietly schemed of ways to get rid of his dots so he could blend in with the crowd. Just to be plain and normal, he thought. So far, vigorous scrubbing with Lava soap was not working. Luckily he didn't make it to the Comet can to scrape them off or bleach them away, whichever came first. It turns out Bud's power was about to shift and he was going to need every one of those freckles.

During second quarter of the football game, as players set their stance on the line of scrimmage, Bud heard the other team say to each other, "Okay, you take the big red head. Knock off a few of those freckles."

"Oh, so I am cool now. Not only that, I am a force to be reckoned with," Bud thought. Puffing his chest to fulfill his newly acquired status, he crouched down and squared his shoulders. "I am going to shove these freckles right in your face," he said to himself. After receiving the handoff, Bud lunged forward for the show down. Running down the defenders that stood in the way, he roared down the field for a touchdown. At the goal posts, Bud threw down the football and threw up his arms into the air in a graceful arc, turning round and round on his hefty feet. Then, continuing his end zone dance, Bud turned his back to the opposing team and swiveled and shimmied up and down to show that, indeed, football was a powerful dance, and now he was king of the football field, freckles and all.

On that very day, Bud stopped scrubbing with Lava soap and put away the can of Comet for good. The very thing that he was embarrassed about had now become his badge of honor. His perceived weakness had turned into a source of power and strength.

SHELLEY THOUGHT SHE WAS A BOY

LIVING NEAR THE LAKOTA SIOUX res-
ervation, we often saw the high cheeked, brown
skinned, Native Americans, whose quiet and re-
served manner was more about brimming with
the unspoken than being meek and passive.
Becoming an Indian in our imagination created
a make believe playground way beyond the confines of our small rural house, four miles outside
of town. Shelley, the second born child, took this
fantasy further until she actually thought she
was an Indian boy, despite her female parts and
stark white skin. She rejected the idea of a tame,
domesticated, indoor lifestyle and chose, instead,
outdoor adventures of living off the land, like
the Indians, which included eating frogs, grasshoppers, and potato bugs. Some of these critters

were still squirming with life when she put them in her mouth. Her Indian spirit was too savage for some neighbors. They locked her out of their house for "telling lies" to their scared children when she spun stories about the perils of a three headed, thousand pound critter outside her bedroom window, which she swore were absolutely true. Skeptical neighbors furrowed their brows and asked her how she knew it was out there. With the conviction of a believer she stated, "I heard it snuffing around." However, Shelley's dangerous trait was not in her stories but what she did with her knife.

Since Mom and Dad were distracted with older sister Celie's medical needs around polio and cataracts, Shelley ran around the countryside mostly unsupervised. She was free to capture grasshoppers, kill lizards, molest porcupines and diminish the frog population as she hunted for food in all shapes and forms. She returned home in Indian time which was whenever she darn well felt like it. Not that anyone noticed anyway.

The usual summer day for Shelley started out by strapping on an Indian breech cloth to cover her private parts down below and a leather sling of bows and arrows over her bare chest. Shelley was blessed with a rare birth defect of an extra rib which lifted one of her shoulders a couple inches higher, giving her a perpetual shrug on one side. The extra rib was so rare that she thought it made her special and probably meant she was supposed to be an angel. The fact that she could not lift her left arm above her shoulder did limit her to killing things closer to the ground.

Uncombed and shaggy hair gave Shelley the look of an unkempt mongrel mutt. A knife was always poised for action in her hand just in case something bolted out in front of her and presented a sudden opportunity for critters to meet their fate. No snake was safe. No chipmunk was too fast to elude being captured, kept captive, and possibly decapitated.

During her early Indian Boy years Shelley ate critters alive. Whenever she was around upturned ground she bent over to study the dark soil. Her hands snatched up a wiggling potato bug, with its fleshy colored body and hefty appendages, and quickly stuffed it into her mouth, whole and alive. Later on, as Shelley matured in her Indian ways, she cooked her meals. Grasshopper legs were pulled off the body and the delicate limbs were toasted in a fry pan. I watched the furry little legs snapping and crackling in the pan.

You eat them like popcorn with a dash of salt," Shelley said. On days she didn't feel like foraging for her meals, she stole her grub from Grandma Lily's pantry just a short jaunt down the road. There was a particular brand of dry dog food that she was very fond of snacking on. Perhaps she was missing iron or protein that the potato bugs and grasshoppers did not provide.

When Shelley felt generous after an abundant day of hunting, she opened up her bag of bounty for viewing. I peered into images of white frog underbellies, blank eyes, and splayed legs that were soon to be her meal. With grey silted hands that had been scraping the creek beds, she plopped a frog down on the cutting board and severed the limbs from the body with her knife. After the dozen or so legs were rinsed, she threw some white flour over them and sprinkled salt and pepper for good measure. The oil popped and spat in the frying pan as the sautéed legs turned golden brown and crispy. Not wanting to be left out of the tasting part of this hunting ritual I restrained from saying, "Hey, I don't think the Indians had enriched flour and a salt and pepper set around their campfire."

Other days, Shelley took on other identities and would proclaim she was to be called "Whip of the World," whatever that was. Then she decided to transform into Tonto or some other hero. The entity known as Shelley disappeared and only Tonto would communicate to family and neighbors.

"Tonto needs a glass of water. I am sorry, you cannot come along. Tonto works alone. I only work for the Lone Ranger." She put her ear to the ground and said, "I hear something from two mile away, Keem-o-sabe."

One day Shelley was thinking of her next disguise and said to Celie, "I sure wish I had glasses."

"You can't have glasses. You don't have cataracts, Celie replied.

"Maybe I'll get cataracts. And then I will have glasses. So there." Shelley snapped back, not to be out done.

"No siree. You have to go out front of the house and get runned over first. And then you have to have an operation where they put needles in your eyes. Only then can you have glasses like mine." Celie confidently knew she had the leading edge on disabilities and said, "So there! Only I can wear glasses." Recognizing that Celie had won in this instance, Shelley quietly walked out of the house and transformed into Tonto for the rest of the day.

For Christmas one year, Mom and Dad gave Shelley what she asked for. A new knife and some mouse traps. They also gave her something extra she wasn't expecting. A ballerina doll. Because she truly believed she was an Indian Boy, she WAS NOT a doll kind of girl. Didn't Mom and Dad have that figured out by now? However, not all was lost. Shelley slashed the doll to test the new knife's sharpness. It passed the test. Then she cut some rope and strapped the ballerina to the post of the clothes line. This was where she perfected her knife throw, improving her precision by piercing the chest, the head, and the crotch. It was a suitable Christmas gift after all.

When the mutilated ballerina doll on the clothes line no longer held her attention, Shelley itched for some adventure. She felt cooped up, restless and bored. This particular winter was long and drawn out. The cold snap, going on two weeks now, stopped all outdoor activity. She wandered through the house and cruised the upstairs dormitory- style bedrooms with rows of beds of our rapidly growing family. Nothing to do up there. Then she fidgeted with some nuts and bolts in the laundry room junk drawer which contained everything that didn't have a proper place. Dissatisfied with the limitations of nuts and bolts, she wandered into the living room.

Shelley spotted her prey. A plump black chair covered with vinyl made to look like leather, with big arms and cushy seat and comfy high back. The smell of new vinyl hung in the air. The price tag was still dangling off the back. It was my mother's only brand new piece of furniture. She had finally reached the end of her patience of staring at worn out and broken down chairs in the living room. From the first moment she set her eyes on it and for months after until she could reckon with Dad that it was money well spent, she yearned for it to adorn her living room. The black chair was not her dream home but it helped fulfill my mother's desire for finer things.

Shelley thought, "I wonder what the sharp knife blade would do to that chair?"

Sitting on the cushioned seat, Shelley ran her fingers over the arm, the seat, and the back, getting a feel for her next move. Stabbing her knife into the stuffed arm, she liked the popping sound of the blade's forceful entry. Pop! Pop! Pop! with each insertion. This was much more interesting than piercing the doll. She stared mesmerized at how the stuffing puffed out of the cuts so beautifully.

Mom walked through the living room moments later to admire her chair. Time froze in place while my mother stared. Her brain synapses momentarily stopped signaling to each other, a form of kindness in a harsh world, giving her mind time to adjust to the new reality. Once the circuits started working again, Mom said this event practically cut Shelley's young life short. Out of the goodness of her heart, Mom decided to let Shelley live. No apologies were exchanged. Indians don't have a term for "I'm sorry". "I'm sorry" is too late for dastardly deeds. "I'm sorry" is an inadequate salve for wounds that cut deep.

One evening, four of us sisters were sitting in the living room fantasizing about who we were going to marry, even though at the age of five, seven, and nine we were too young to choose or be chosen. This was the first moment in our lives when we considered boys as potentially more than playmates and targets to pick on. Celie wanted to marry the oldest neighbor boy as soon as she was old enough. "I hope he waits for me to grow up," Celie murmured. Then she added, "It's too bad that all the other cute boys I know are my cousins.

Shelley asked, "Do I have to get married when I grow up?"

"Well, no," Mom said, looking up from her mending.

Shelley's eyes filled with tears and wet streams rolled down her cheeks. She choked out her words, "I don't want to get married..... because..... I'm afraid... I won't be able to find my way back home.

Can I have children without getting married?" Shelley asked, after a long pause, calculating her future.

"No," Mom replied.

A neighbor girl who joined the conversation asked, "If Shelley doesn't get married, can't she even have a little mentally retarded child?"

"No, you have to get married before you have any child," Mom asserted with authority.

Dad, sitting at the dining room table and playing Solitaire, chimed in, "Forget about marriage. We have a different problem. Do you know that we drink more milk in this household than any restaurant serves in town? That is what the milk man told me when he dropped off our milk. We use so much milk that I am afraid we will have to trade in a few kids for a milk cow."

"Let's trade Celie off," Shelley quickly suggested.

"But we have a lot more money invested in Celie. Maybe we should trade you off," Mom said.

"But Mom, I want to stay here," Shelley said, hiccupping from withholding a sob. Her face contorted and another round of tears flowed down her cheeks.

In time, when she ripened into an adult, Shelley would get married and her fears would be confirmed. Indeed, she would not be able to find her way back home. Shelley would continue choosing the path of the lone brave.

Perhaps she is out in the world now telling stories about a three thousand pound critter with three heads that she heard snuffin' around. Maybe she will find her way back home one day as an Indian brave would, traveling full circle, ending up where she began, but with a new vision of who she is and where she has been.

A vision could draw from the wisdom of all four corners of the earth with a new story emerging out of it. A different story that would allow for failings and short comings, her own and others, with the understanding that hardships and betrayals can become our teachers.

I imagine a wise Indian chief sharing a story with the newly initiated brave called Paleface With Uneven Shoulders, as they sit together near the riverbank under the full moon. Handing the peace pipe over to the new brave, he begins, "The river water flows. The water is never the same. This river that we drank from yesterday is not the same river we drink from today. That river of life flows through us as well in the same way. Everything changes. Nothing stays the same." As the campfire embers die down, the ashes are scattered to the four corners, signaling the end of this day and all that has happened, for tomorrow is brand new day.

SORDID STORIES OF AN ORDINARY FAMILY

AFTERWORD

*We were a strange little band of characters
trudging through life sharing diseases and
toothpaste, coveting one another's desserts,
hiding shampoo, borrowing money, locking each
other out of our rooms, inflicting pain and kissing
to heal it in the same instant, loving, laughing,
defending, and trying to figure out the common
thread that bound us all together.*
~Erma Bombeck

"You know what has hurt me the most?" Dad asked Shelley.

Shelley contemplated his question for a moment. "Let's see. I don't do drugs. I don't sleep around. I don't recall any felony or misdemeanor. Hmm. What is my big crime Dad?"

I read somewhere that each person possesses an average of fifteen hundred rules about how we think the world should be and how people should behave in it. Making matters worse, most of our rules are unspoken and therefore unknown by others. Yet, if someone does something that violates one of our rules, we feel as if an agreement was broken and hold the other person ransom to our feeling wounded, even if they may not know about the rule or might not agree with it in the first place.

"I am bothered by the fact that you registered

Democrat," Dad replied with certainty. Operating under the strength of conviction of his belief, if he felt strongly about something, he assumed his opinion must be right. Shelley had apparently broken one of Dad's rules by signing up for a political affiliation different from his. If turning traitor and defecting to the Democratic Party hurt the most, what other rules had she broken along the way? Feeling righteously wronged, Dad sat in his chair sulking while Shelley retreated into silence and got up to leave.

Perhaps Dad was missing a sense of a common thread within the family, and the fact that Shelley broke one of his rules was a sign to him that the family was unraveling at the seams.

Rules form, lots of them. Like cells, they just keep replicating and splitting off and mutating. Some of them change as they get tested and evolve. Some of them just stay put and survive and keep on going no matter what the circumstances-- rain, snow, or shine. They are our survival map for making sense of the world, a world that doesn't always make sense. Wondering how rules affect the feeling of having a common thread, I thought I'd take a crack at uncovering some rules in my family, particularly about dealing with challenges that arise within our family.

"Forgiving others for events that hurt us," according to Shelley, "is a very personal journey and no one knows our answers but ourselves. For me, forgiving doesn't mean forgetting because remembering is important in order to learn."

"I'm lucky I have tunnel vision and that it is good for some things!" Celie crowed with pride over her ability to be blind to injustices. "Because I saw life through a magnifying glass, I had to stay so focused on what was right in front of me. I guess I developed selective vision of seeing only what I wanted to see. I didn't have a wide angle lens to include the bad. I like to think that just because someone screws up and does bad things doesn't make them a bad person," she added as she bumped into a chair near her that she hadn't seen.

"Grudgesth are an ignorant wasthe of time," Kristy proclaimed, "and they stheal your joy. Nothing, I mean nothing isth worth holding a grudge." Kristy continued on with the conviction of a believer. "How can you appreciate a good man the way they destherve to be apprecthiated if you haven't been betrayed by a sthcoundrel? Besthides we get to develop sthrength of character through those hardsthipsth. Thosthe troublesth I have encountered have made me the amazing and ctharming persthon that I am," she said smiling and flexing her biceps.

"Well, you need a big heart to survive a family," Carol reflected. "You can't choose your family. You can fire your friends and hire them for their qualities, but you just inherit your family. They are going to do things that bug the shit out of you, and when you have a big family, there is going to be a lot of stuff to work out. For me, I think forgiveness in a family is very important.

They are worth it. When I have to work on something to forgive, I talk about it a lot to anyone who will listen, then I analyze the hell out of it, over and over in my head, and then I find ways to cope with it. There is one thing, though, that I have to say about a gap in my upbringing. It would have been nice to have been told by my parents that it's good to see the good in people, but you don't have to marry them. It could have saved me some problems. It's okay. I forgive them."

"I no longer wait for my sisters to return the favors of dishes I did for them," Bud sighed, and then chuckled. "I was promised 'tomorrow' and 'tomorrow' never came. Getting over disappointment got ingrained into my daily life until getting over things became part of my nature. Gina, you threw a wood block at me and hit me on the head, just to show off for the guys in the post yard. That knot on my forehead burned and throbbed, and even drew a little blood, and you just laughed at my pain, and then whooped a battle cry over your deadly accuracy," Bud stated, without a hint of judgment. Just stating the facts.

"Is it too late to say I'm sorry?" I asked.

"My memories have always had a short span, so you are off the hook," he replied. "It's all good, it's all good." Bud added.

"Gina, you offered an apology a few years ago for "everything you ever did, intentional and un-intentional, and I accepted," Lisa replied, even though there are some other hurts that haven't been resolved. "I'm not saying that an apology has to come forth before forgiveness can be granted, but it helps. But I do agree that it is important to forgive or a family will turn sordid."

"I have finally forgiven you Mom," I said as we sat across the table.

"For what?" she asked, looking up from her crossword puzzle.

"For making me eat those 'pigs in a blanket' that you served at dinner. I hated the dryness of the dough wrapped around the hot dog smothered with the mustard sauce. The bitterness of the sauce assaulted my sensitive taste buds. Besides, I have always hated hot dogs. Swallowing hard to choke down every bite was like being forced to eat bile. Your only response was, 'This isn't a short order cook house. You will eat the food I serve or go hungry.' But it's okay. I am over the fact that you didn't care one bit about my food preferences."

And then we hugged.

"Well, that's good you let go of that, Gina, because grudges give you wrinkles," Mom said, "and will give you constipation. Lucky for me," she added, "I got a regular constitution."

After hearing some of the different rules from my family, I am wondering if shared rules have to be the common thread, with everyone's precious dogma going in the same direction. Looking at our family, our common threads may be loosely woven and not seem so plentiful if you look at our various rule books. However, apparently there is enough of a knit to keep us coming together and enjoying each other's company. Could it be that the common

thread of our bunch of knock-kneed, gimpy, nearly
blind, freckled, accident prone, highly spirited,
and independent individuals comes down to one
overarching rule-- that family is worth enduring
the hurts and hassles, and so we are compelled
to follow that rule by simply coming back to each
other to offer and receive love, which may involve
the same person who has hurt us in the past?
I wonder.

www.ingramcontent.com/pod-product-compliance
Lightning Source LLC
Chambersburg PA
CBHW052215270326
41931CB00011B/2355